YANKEE SUMMER:
The Way We Were

YANKEE SUMMER:
The Way We Were

Growing up in a rural Vermont in the 1930s

by

Lewis Hill

ISBN: 1-58820-031-0

1stBooks - rev. 9/5/00

Contents

Chapters

Introduction

When the ladies of our summer community started wearing shorts, smoking cigarettes and driving cars, many of the local women felt the end of the world couldn't be far away. Certainly the Lord would not let such happenings go on for long.

But gradually nearly everyone except dear old Nellie Ingalls became less upset at the changes and the folks from "away" didn't seem to be quite so strange any more. True, they played golf, sailed boats, wore white suits and funny hats, talked weird, wore wrist watches, read "foreign" newspapers and magazines, and carried tennis rackets around a lot. The young crowd drove open top roadsters, let their arms and sometimes their legs hang out over the doors, and made, what seemed to us, a lot of noise.

I feel lucky to have lived enough in the pre-World War II era to experience much of what our ancestors had endured. I visited an old time working lumber camp once, my family made soap, vinegar, butter, and raised a variety of animals and poultry. I was also fortunate that our town contained a neat collection of rock solid Yankees, old Scots, new French Canadian farmers from north of the border as well as the big group of city folks that invaded our town each summer. In the next town, a group of quite different Italian, Scottish, and French granite workers provided us with an exciting Saturday night whenever we wanted one. All of them affected our lives in various ways.

In the thirties most of the country, including the rural areas, were very depressed. By living on a farm we certainly did better than the poor people in the cities. Everyone here still had the survival skills that our ancestors had developed, and we never had been used to prosperity. We raised most of our own food, cut our fuel, and had generations of experience of dealing with things that consistently go wrong.

It was also a good time to be young. Unlike the grownups, we didn't feel threatened by the new ideas and inventions that were appearing, and none of us had any memories of better times. None of our neighbors were any better off than we, and we didn't envy the more prosperous summer visitors who had to spend most of the year in cities. The radio now kept us informed of a world that we had known of only in our geography books, and finally we could begin to almost feel a part of it.

A large lake had brought the earliest settlers to our town. The fish furnished abundant food during the first years of clearing land before they could plant crops. The outlet furnished power to run a sawmill, gristmill, shingle mill, sash and blind industry, wagon factory, and several other shops. Only the sawmill and wagon factory were working when I was growing up, and folks from the cities had completely bought the entire area that ringed the beautiful lake except for a small public beach. If we went to the village in summer we heard a Babel of New York, Princeton, Hartford, Boston, and Philadelphia accents.

The "foreigners" not only brought in strange words, but also curious customs, some quite offensive to the century-old traditions of the natives. The new people got very close to people's faces when they talked and some waved their hands vigorously as they spoke in a way that made the Yankees nervous.

Whenever things got too comfortable, a preacher came to town with a camp meeting to warn everyone of the imminent ending of the world because of our immoral ways, and everyone thought he was talking about the newcomers. He would yell about the Chicago Fire, San Francisco earthquake, tidal waves, wars, and threats of wars as signs of the soon to arrive Armageddon. Some of the prophets would even set the day and hour for the trumpet to sound, and one of them urged his listeners to dress in white and sit on their roofs to await.

Of great interest to me was the one lady spiritualist who was left from the great movement that had swept the country earlier. She held seances, and put people in touch with their dead relatives. I always wanted to go and watch a table rise slowly in the air, but never had the chance. We did hear the story, probably made up, of one man who wanted to contact his dead wife through a medium. Finally he got through and asked her what Heaven was like. "Well, its nice," she admitted, but it's not Vermont."

No longer was our town all Congregationalists and Methodists. We now had Roman Catholics who held a mass in Latin, and listened to a sermon in French each Sunday. A group of Seventh Day Adventists celebrated their Sabbath on Saturday, and sometimes upset their neighbors by haying, plowing, and cutting wood on Sunday.

The summer crowd didn't try to convert us to any new religions, but some of their customs appealed to the younger set, more than their elders wanted. Farm boys began going without shirts and caps, and wives began to drive cars. Pipe smoking men who had previously considered cigarettes a sissy habit, began buying the so-called coffin nails, but always carefully explained that it was only to save the constant relighting of their pipes.

We kids were fascinated with the airplanes that occasionally landed on the lake or in fields near the village. It seemed to us that the world promised by Popular Science, the Tom Swift books, and Buck Rogers might now be within reach.

We were also learning some isms-fascism, communism, socialism, and Nazism. People were worried that Germany and Japan would fight the coming war with death rays, deadly germs, nerve gas, and fantastic explosives from dive bombers. Newspapers warned about the Yellow Peril, whereby billions of Orientals would take over the world. The German Bund was becoming a new threatening force in the cities, and they were setting up camps throughout the country to train the youth in "the new order." All things for which we feared our country was unprepared.

But most of this had little effect on our area. Europe was still far away, Japan even further, and much closer were hard winters, mortgages, poor farm markets, and the host of the tribulations that, we were told, "human flesh is heir to."

But it was summer vacation, and the dreaded high school was two months away. Beyond that, who knew what? Would we follow the traditions of ancestors, or be swept up in something quite new, something for which no one we knew seemed ready for. Some days it all seemed exciting, and we could hardly wait. But at others it seemed more than a little frightening.

Chapter 1

The Merry Month of May-The Rare Days of June

"I'd enjoy spring a dern sight more if I weren't always thinking about how winter will be arriving only a few weeks later." Rolland Whitaker.

Spring never busted out all over in northern Vermont. It teased. Two warm days in March got us all excited and hopeful that maybe, just maybe, spring would come early just like we heard it had 50 years ago. But winter invariably returned after the false start, jarring us, as well as the early arriving robins. Eventually, in late April, the snowstorms, clouds, and dampness began to give way to the bright sunny days of May. As the Yankees laid aside their heavy boots and wool coats, hats, and gloves, someone always pointed out that, in our region, there was lots of difference between the first day of spring and the first spring day.

Like the weather, our neighbors changed in the spring. During the long, cold, dark winters, they tended to get sullen, and many developed all sorts of ailments. Dr. Allen once said that as soon as he could get his patients out to grass, most of them would recover. Mark Bechtold was a prime example of the folks who went through a dormant period. He was a pleasant enough person through the spring, summer, and fall months, but he became more and more crabby as winter went on, and by town meeting in March he had become such a terrible grouch that everyone hoped he wouldn't show up in town. Storekeepers and the postman hated to see him coming, since he picked a row with everyone from the minister to the boy who walked past his house on the way to school.

With the first warm May day, though, Mark's personality changed. Folks who were pretending they hadn't seen him when he was buying seeds at the local store were flabbergasted at his wide grin and friendly remarks. Although his blood didn't start moving quite as fast as the sap in the maple trees, it flowed as soon as he felt some positive signs of spring.

Like Mark, I loved spring. It was the end of my last year in the one room school where it seemed as if I had spent most of my 12 years, and I felt on the verge of a new life. I was acutely aware, that year, of spring stirring on our old farm. Most calves were born in springtime, and their bleating voices echoed throughout the barn. As soon as they were born, the youngsters were able to walk on thin, wobbly legs and they seemed surprised at the world they had suddenly encountered.

Our yard was filled with baby chicks toddling behind their cackling mothers, cats with litters of new kittens, and many birds flying about, busily feeding their growing offspring. Supplying food and protecting the new lives was a full-time job for the mothers, and for us, too. Since our small poultry flock ran free, we had to be on the lookout for weasels, skunks, hawks, owls, rats, and foxes, who were also very hungry. It was one of my jobs to button all the birds into the hen house each night, and to get the mother hens into their various little chicken coops, lined up like a little village. As the days got longer the flock had little interest in going to bed early, so I had to track them down, and entice them to bed with a trail of corn.

The White Leghorn broody hens sat on their eggs for 3 weeks to hatch their chicks. One year, my brother decided to raise some ducks and bought 4 duck eggs from one of his friends. He carefully tucked them under one hen who had shown considerable interest in motherhood by clucking and ruffling her feathers. She didn't seem to mind her strange-looking offspring when they hatched out, but when they jumped into their water dish and started splashing about, she squawked enough to raise the dead. When they got a bit older, one day I saw them all swim out into a little pond made by the melting snow in back of our barn. The mother hen sounded like Chicken Little screaming that the sky was falling. Even though the biddy, which was what we called a hen, couldn't understand her wayward brood, she dutifully looked after them and tried to keep them together as a family long after they were nearly twice her size.

2

I stayed outdoors as late as possible in the long spring evenings. More birds arrived from the South each day, and spring sounds wafted through the air. Peepers sang noisily from every little spring pond on the farm, and bullfrogs occasionally lent a deep, bass chug-a-lug to the soprano chorus. In the valley below our house the little brook that murmured peacefully most of the year roared noisily as tons of snow melted in the woods. Now and then an owl hooted, and occasionally I heard the scary, unearthly scream of a bobcat which effectively kept me from venturing into the woods at twilight.

Since I was the youngest of my large family, several of my older brothers and sisters had already left home to make their own ways in the world, so our farmhouse held nicely those of us who remained: Ma, one brother, one sister, and me. Another brother lived on an adjoining farm with his family and we operated the two properties together. Since my father had died soon after I was born, my mother and siblings now had the responsibility not only of the dairy farm, but also of seeing that I had plenty of proper "fetching up", even if some of them didn't come home often. The youngest child was traditionally spoiled, but, my kinfolks had apparently never heard of that tradition.

By the time I arrived, my mother had become very experienced, not only at fetching up children, but at managing all the household chores of a farm wife. To Ma, spring was not a time to go bird-watching or gather wildflowers. May was the month for spring cleaning which did not mean a perfunctory once-over but a thorough scrubbing and uprooting, from cellar to attic. If sickness or any other important reason caused spring house cleaning to be missed, some women felt it was necessary to clean their entire house twice in the fall.

Ma, a stickler for tradition, felt that every closet should be emptied, as should every drawer, all books should be taken from their shelves and dusted, and any leftover produce taken from the cellar. Saturdays, when I was home from school, I was enlisted to help move heavy trunks and furniture. This spring chore was not nearly as distasteful to me as cleaning out the stinking pig pens or picking stones out of a dusty, newly-harrowed field. Still, I felt each year, that my ancestors who had settled there more than a century earlier had saved far too much old junk for apparently no other reason than to move it twice a year.

My mother also felt that all our winter clothing and most other worldly goods should be washed and "aired out", and when I came home from school on a sunny day the front yard looked as if we were having an auction. Rugs, furs, woolens, and bedclothes were thrown over chairs.. Our winter coats, shirts, socks, and hats were hung on the clotheslines, as well as the smelly horse blankets and the hairy buffalo robe that kept us warm when riding in the sleigh during the winter. Even the nails on the walls of our veranda supported airing winter garments. It was fun to drive to the village in the spring and take inventory along the way of all our neighbors' garments and bedclothes spread over their clotheslines and chairs in the front yard.

Although occasionally I helped bring in the clothes at the end of the day, I was more hindrance than help because I liked to slip on the grownups' heavy old coonskin and sheepskin-lined winter coats, and it was fun to fool around with the fur gloves and muffs that were still carefully preserved, even though no one ever wore them any more. After a thorough airing each spring, Ma packed them away and we wouldn't see them again until the following May.

They all had to be protected from the ravenous moth larvae that chewed holes in woolens and furs. After Ma had emptied all the summer clothes from the upstairs closets, brought them downstairs, and filled the empty spaces with winter woolens, she carefully spread fresh mothballs and cedar boughs amongst them. I envisioned thousands of moths armed with little knives and forks ready to devour any woolens left unprotected, but because of her care we never found any holes in our winter socks or breeches. Since I disliked the heavy aroma of moth balls, I tried to stay out of the house by volunteering instead for the job of going into the nearby woods to clip off cedar boughs that were also used as moth repellents.

Before Ma put the winter clothes away, she checked them for holes and looked over mine for size, since I was growing fast. The general stores and catalogs had sales in the spring, and we tried to lay in necessities as soon as the muddy roads dried enough to get over them.

Each spring, in addition to doing the thorough scrubbing, most women in the neighborhood painted and wallpapered a few rooms, since at last it was warm enough for windows to be left open. We usually bought our paint and wallpaper by mail-order from Sears Roebuck or Montgomery Ward in late winter so the mailman could deliver it before the roads broke up. Sometimes neighboring women got together to do such work, and a woman who was good at painting would often swap jobs with another who was clever at hanging wallpaper. My mother preferred to do it all herself and I was always impressed with the way she made large batches of gooey paste out of flour and water and was able to make the long strips of paper stick to the ceiling.

All of us were involved with spring cleaning. Meals were sometimes late because it was hard to interrupt a paint job, and everyone was needed to move beds and other furniture out of any rooms being redone. I liked to yell loudly in the empty rooms to hear the hollow echoes, and to hang out the open windows and soak up the smells and sounds of spring.

That spring, as usual, we took off the double windows and storm doors we'd struggled to put on in the fall, and installed the window screens and screen doors. We also had to remove the banking from around the house foundation. Each fall we got a load of shavings from a nearby shingle mill for this purpose. Spring was also the time to clean the two chimneys and stovepipes, and to clean and put blacking on the three wood stoves.

My brother also cleaned our spring, a quarter-mile away, and let the air out of the water pipe that had built up over the winter, but I could only help with these chores after school and on Saturdays. Since winter dominated our lives for at least five months each year, somebody always wondered about what the people in Hawaii and Mexico were doing while we spent so much time preparing for it, struggling in it, and getting over it, but no one I knew ever went to find out.

It seemed as if there was never an end to the farm work that had to be done promptly. "Got your spring's work done?" was a common greeting among both men and women, and of course, no one ever admitted he had. Bill Peterson admitted that he liked driving around the back country on Sunday afternoons because "if you go far enough you're bound to find someone who is further behind in his work than you be." Then he'd add, "Course sometimes I have to go to the next town for that." I spent quite a bit of time envying the boys my age in the village whose families worked in the mill or store, because they could go fishing or woodchuck hunting with them on Saturdays. They didn't have to plant corn, spread manure, or fix fences. Also, I didn't like cattle and knew they weren't called "bossy" without reason. Although some farmers seemed to cherish their cows and named each one, I suspected from talking with my schoolmates that I was not the only one who resented how they dominated my life.

Anything from cleaning out the manure that had piled up all winter in the barn basement, to cutting a supply of wood for boiling maple sap the following year was considered "spring work." We had to spread all of winter's big piles of manure on the newly thawed fields before the grass grew more than a few inches tall. Planting seeds at the right time was the most frustrating because of our unpredictable weather, but we all were told over and over with ominous certainty that if we didn't get the fields of oats and corn and the vegetable garden planted on time, the next winter would be a rough one for man and beast.

As soon as green grass appeared we let the cattle out of the barn where they'd spent the winter. Before that could happen, however, we had to repair miles of fences. Only a few rail fences remained by the late thirties, and most of our fences consisted of four strands of barbed wire, attached to a post every 8 feet or so. Each year many strands were broken by the settling of the frozen crusts of snow, and others rusted away. The tips of the cedar posts beneath the soil rotted after a few years, too, and we always found fences in the woods wrecked by trees that had fallen during the winter.

Before fixing the fences, we sawed the old split rails that had once been our fences into posts and sharpened the ends that were to be pounded into the wet, soft earth. Fixing fences took us into some of the wooded sections of the 200 acres that I never saw any other time, but it was a struggle to carry the posts and heavy rolls of barbed wire far into the woods where we couldn't go with horses. There were often surprises that made the trips fun, however. One morning we encountered a newborn fawn that its mother had tried to hide in some clumps of sprouting ferns while she went searching for food, and occasionally there was a partridge with a brood of little ones. The mother always pretended to have a broken wing and tried to lead us away from her fuzzy chicks. One day I found sap dripping from a broken branch on a silver birch tree. Sampling it, I found it had a sweet birch flavor, like birch beer, and decided that the next year I would tap a birch after the maple season was done. Sometimes, deep in the woods, we would run into frost when we were driving posts, even in June, and I wondered if it might be permafrost that signaled the beginning of a new Ice Age.

The work of maintaining fences between neighboring properties had been agreed upon long ago, and each owner was expected to keep his half in good repair. The proper way was to measure the fence by pacing it off, then each farmer would face his side of the fence, and each one had to maintain the half on his right. Sometime these arrangements caused difficulties when new landowners who didn't have cattle or horses saw no reason why they should be responsible for fencing out their neighbors' herds. The lawyers made a good income off these frequent disagreements but also tried hard to get the neighbors to settle after they had made all the money they felt they could. They wanted to make sure that no case would reach a court where they couldn't be sure of the outcome. They all knew that the ancient ordinance required the sharing of building and maintaining fences defined a proper fence as one that was "horse high and sheep tight,"-a much more elaborate one than cattle needed.

When our fences were finally inspected and repaired, I helped let out the cattle. After being shut in the barn all winter, the cows were as happy to 'get out to pasture' as we were to let them go. I was always surprised to see our huge Holsteins run in circles and jump into the air, cavorting like calves at their new freedom. We worried a bit that their little-used winter legs might break in their merriment, but they never did.

Each spring we took the heifers, young female cattle, to a pasture nearly a mile away for the summer. The land belonged to a neighbor who no longer kept animals and was glad to rent it out. The grazing gave him a little income, and it also kept down the small trees that were forever creeping onto abandoned land. The arrangement meant, however, that we had to repair what seemed like miles of additional fences every spring, and we always had our hands full as we drove the frisky young heifers along the road past the gardens, cattle, and dogs of several neighbors. Each dog felt compelled to bark and defend its territory against our critters as they passed by.

We had one pasture near the barn where the cows spent the night which we called the 'night pasture', and another, farther away, was the 'day pasture'. Twice a day, night and morning, I had to round up about thirty milking cows in the pastures and, with the help of the dog, drive them to the barn. Often, there were one or two who wanted to give me a hard time, and they would run the other way, just to be contrary, but Peggy, with a few barks, got them quickly back in line. Old timers liked to tell about their encounters with bears while they were chasing cows in their youth, but since I never even saw a bear track, those stories didn't bother me. Cows, like most animals, are creatures of habit and most contented in a predictable routine. Each had its own stanchion in the barn and went to it faithfully. They also liked to be fed and milked at regular times and gave less milk whenever the schedule was changed.

Unlike some of our neighbors, we didn't let our bull outside except for mating purposes. Bulls were always unpredictable, and stories about injuries from them were commonplace. Gestation period for cows is about nine and a half months, and farmers were beginning to adjust their breeding patterns so that not all their young calves were born in the spring. Each cow gave milk for nine or ten months following birth, and was then 'dry' for two or three, while her calf was nearing the time of birth.

Each cow felt that birthing was a private affair, and she tried to have her calf as far away from civilization as possible, often hiding in the woods or tall bushes. We sometimes spent hours or even days searching before we located the missing pair and brought them to the barn. Many times I walked within a few feet of the animals hidden in their private nursery and never noticed them. Usually, after being found, the new mother was ready to come back for some grain and water but occasionally, if she resented being taken in, we had to carry the calf to get her to follow us home. After a few days of confinement though, the cow was ready for a familiar routine again.

We had four horses most of the time. My oldest brother liked them and, like many farmers, considered them very close to human. Not only did he and most of his horse-loving friends remember the names of every animal they had ever owned, but also the names of most of those belonging to their neighbors. Whenever they got together, horses was not only the main subject discussed, but often the only one. Bill Buckley, especially, bragged constantly about how clever all his horses had been, but I never heard any such praise for his wife or children.

Our big work horses must have sensed that I wasn't very fond of them, because I was often kicked, bitten, stepped on, and tossed off their backs. I knew their names, but hadn't bothered to learn all the proper horse terminology and could never remember if 'gee' or 'haw' meant to turn right. I'd been told many times that I must always approach a horse from the left, but I discovered early that a horse didn't really care which side I came from, as long as it wasn't startled.

My reputation with the neighbors as an animal ignoramus peaked when, on the way to school one morning, I met our neighbor, Mr. Coomer, who allowed he'd just lost his horse. I told him I had seen a strange horse on our roadside.

"What color is it?" he demanded.

"Brown," I replied helpfully.

"Well, what kind of brown? Bay, chocolate, chestnut, what?"

Chestnuts didn't grow in our country, so I had never seen one, and had always thought that a bay was sort of blue, like a lake. Chocolate seemed more like a flavor than a color.

9

"Looked brown to me," was all I could manage. The old guy sputtered about my ignorance as he left to pick up his horse of undetermined color, and he mentioned it every time he saw me for the rest of his life.

The next big chore in May, after fixing fences, was to plow and harrow the fields in preparation for planting. Most farmers believed that hayfields had to be renewed every few years by plowing and seeding, and they acted accordingly. Only a few maintained that they could keep their fields producing forever by fertilizing, but I wasn't lucky enough to have brothers who shared that belief.

Plowing came first, usually in the fall, but if the weather was too wet or snowy, the farmers did it in spring. My oldest brother drove the team of horses with the reins tied around his waist, so he could use both hands to hold and steer the plow. The sharp end of the plow dug into the earth, grabbed it, and turned the soil completely over. At the end of the row, he unlatched the plowshare beneath the plow and flipped it over so he could plow another furrow coming back. He turned the new furrow into the ditch made by the previous one, and so on, until the top layer of the entire field was bottom side up. Plowing was slow, hard work for both man and beast, particularly on the stony land in our town. The next process, always in the spring, was to disk the soil with a wheel harrow to pulverize it, again using the team of horses. At that point we had to pick up what seemed like millions of stones that were strewn everywhere.

One of my brothers was very proud of his planting ability and expertly flung the oats and grass seed off the ends of his fingers and covered a field evenly with seed. He kept track of where he had been by watching his footprints in the soft earth. The next job was to till the seed into the soft soil with a spiked tooth harrow, pulled by the team. Then he smoothed the field with a wooden platform called a dray, that looked somewhat like a wide boat.

After a rain, the sprouting oats transformed the brown earth into a carpet of light, lush green. The oats were the 'catch' crop for the hay seeds, because they sprouted quickly and protected the timothy, red top fescues, and clover seeds that grew more slowly. These new grasses were to furnish our hay for the next several years.

Of all the farm chores I didn't enjoy, stone picking topped the list. People who had been in Quebec, just across the Canadian border only a few miles from our farm, reported seeing acres of level fields with hardly a stone or rock in sight. It was hard for me to understand why the glacier had cleaned off their land so thoroughly and deposited tons and tons of rocks on our hilly slopes. Each winter someone always cheerfully predicted that another glacier was headed in our direction with another big load of rocks.

No one ever told me that stones had a sex life, but I was well-acquainted with the procreation of farm animals and was convinced they did, since a new crop invariably appeared each time anyone plowed a field. Rocks were not only good at begetting, but they seemed to increase in size, as well. I decided that they, like trees, must need soil to go forth and multiply, because when piled in heaps or placed carefully in walls, they didn't change a bit.

We tugged, pushed, and pulled the stones, rolling the bigger ones onto a flat, sled-like set of boards called a stone boat. The smaller stones we lifted up and threw into a dump cart, the highest vehicle we owned. It had two back wheels about five feet high, and by removing a steel rod we could easily dump the entire load at the edge of the field, after we had tossed in all the stones the horses could easily pull.

Although none of us had much control over the farm schedule, stone picking, it seemed to me, always took place on the hottest, windiest, driest day of spring. After an hour, both we and the horses were completely covered with dirt. The black fly season that usually coincided with the stone picking was just one more annoyance. In school that spring our teacher had read aloud James Russell Lowell's poem:

"What is so rare as a day in June?
Then, if ever, come perfect days."

I was certain that Mr. Lowell had never picked stones on a hot June day when the black flies were biting, or he wouldn't have had such fond memories of that month. June was bug

11

season as well as stone season. Larger flies began to breed as soon as the spring sun warmed both the manure that we'd spread on the fields and the horse manure left on the roads from winter traffic. Except for the deer flies that bit with a vengeance, most of them didn't bite like the black flies, but they seemed determined to take up residence in our home and barn. The old wire screens we installed each spring seldom fit tightly in the doors and windows, and Ma warned us repeatedly not to hold the screen doors open any longer than was necessary to dash through. Luckily, because days were extra long at that time of year, we went to bed before our lights could attract the flood of moths, June bugs, and other insects waiting for their chance to come storming in.

One chore that was mine each spring was to take the winter's rubbish to our dump, a quarter mile from the house. Like most farms, we had our own dumping spot and, like many others, it was located near a brook on a rocky slope that couldn't be used for farming purposes and had already collected nearly a century of castaways. There were no regulations against dumping rubbish, and ours caused no pollution because we didn't throw away any hazardous materials.

Discarding anything at all was not a normal practice for anyone in my family, so there wasn't much for me to transport most years. We burned our paper, mended and recycled clothing, and delivered any leftover food each day to the chickens, pigs, and pets. Consequently, my wheelbarrrow load usually consisted of a couple of liniment or vanilla bottles, broken china, fractured window glass, old screens, discarded stovepipe, and other unusable things that surfaced during spring cleaning. I liked going to the dump because I was alone there and could throw rocks at anything breakable that wasn't already broken. I imagined what I could do if I ever got the .22 rifle I'd been admiring in the catalogs.

The dump was a good place to daydream, too. Just below it was the fast-running brook where I could see the remains of the old grist mill my great-grandfather had operated when he first lived on our farm. It was fun to imagine how the wagons had brought corn and wheat to the mill when it was operating in a spring just like this one, with the brook full of water. I could almost hear the two huge stones grinding various grains into flour, corn meal, or the cracked corn that people fed to their chickens and other animals.

I found part of the old dam, mostly disappeared after more than a century of spring floods, and imagined where the wooden flume had carried the water to the overshot water wheel. Standing on one of the old mill stones that was still there, I wondered how long it took to cut such a perfect circle out of a rough granite boulder and then to carve a hole through the center for the shaft.

From those reveries it wasn't difficult to go back even further and wonder what the woods looked like before anyone cut any of the huge trees or built roads. Did bears, moose, and mountain lions pass by this spot and did beavers dam up the brook? Did any twelve year old Indian boy ever sit on a rock here, like me, wondering about the past and dreaming about what might happen in the future?

After the spring's muddy roads had dried up, the road crew began to repair the winter and spring damage, and I liked to watch the grader go by. Four husky horses drew the four-wheeled contraption with a blade beneath it. The road commissioner, who was the boss, stood on a platform on the machine, drove the horses, and worked the various wheels and levers that manipulated the blade. Four or five men with potato forks and long handled shovels followed the grader, picking the loosened rocks out of the road and throwing them to the sides. They repaired the water bars that had been built to divert any water running down the roads into the ditches beside the roads. The older folks often referred to these bars as "kiss-me-quicks," because in horse and buggy days, the jolt when the buggy hit the bar was supposed to throw a couple together, and if the boy was alert, he could steal a quick kiss before the chaperone noticed. Although the bars were of no hindrance to the slow moving buggies of previous years, they did annoy people in cars, and were gradually removed.

Most men who worked on the roads were either old-timers who no longer farmed or younger men who did road work year-round. Some were hard to understand because the younger ones often had heavy French-Canadian accents, and many of the older men spoke with a rich Yankee dialect more pronounced than the one I usually heard.

The road commissioner left the grader beside our barn one night when they were working in our neighborhood, and he drove his horses home with a wagon he had brought earlier. It was a great opportunity for me to inspect the machine, and when my brothers weren't looking, I hopped on and began to push the various wheels and levers that controlled the blade. Since I had never been exposed to much machinery, I had to figure out the mechanical movements that controlled everything. When I had to leave for chores, I tried to remember where I had found the blade to begin with, but after half an hour of playing I wasn't too sure. It seemed like a good idea to be out of sight when the commissioner returned in the morning, and I was relieved when I heard the grader going up the hill. I was also glad that I hadn't accidentally let it roll down the slope where it had been parked.

The biggest excitement of that spring was a forest fire that broke out on a hot June afternoon when we were picking stones. It was only a couple of miles from our farm–far too close to ignore. The telephone operator had spread the word by ringing a long ring on all the nearby party lines, the usual signal for an emergency, and in only a few minutes many men and boys were on their way. We quickly grabbed some shovels and followed our neighbors' cars toward a pillar of smoke that was billowing up into the blue western sky.

I had never been near a forest fire before and had no idea what to do, nor did most of the others. Finally a few men from the village appeared who had fought blazes before. They told us that one can never put out a forest fire, but the idea was to keep it from spreading by beating it out with shovels around the edges, and moving anything burnable out of the way.

When Shorty Fenn arrived, everybody groaned a little. He was a pompous little man who picked up his feet and put them down firmly when he walked, and he immediately began telling all of us what to do. Nobody paid any attention to him, but that didn't bother him a trifle. He marched along the fire line, bossing

14

everyone but not doing anything himself. Knowing Shorty, we were all aware that for years in the future he would be telling everyone that "the whole dang town woulda burned ta ashes ifen it hadn't been for me, 'cause I was the only one there who knew anything."

After we'd worked for an hour or so and were getting very hot and thirsty, a contractor brought in a tractor. It dug a wide path around the fire so the flames couldn't burn across it, though it didn't stop the stifling smoke. Finally the blaze began to simmer down and we walked back to the road where some women from the village had set up a folding table with sandwiches, coffee, and, best of all, some water. I felt very relieved to know finally that the fire probably wouldn't reach our woods.

In the late afternoon the man who'd been appointed town forest fire warden arrived from a roofing job he was doing in the next town. Although there wasn't much fire left, he brought out pumps, fire rakes and shovels that he kept on hand. Then he tore around, inspecting everything, and directed us to dig out the little smoldering hot spots that still persisted. At the same time, however, he was nervously lighting one cigarette after another and tossing them away, starting little conflagrations wherever he walked. Finally the man who was following him and stamping out the fires he'd started asked him whose side he was on, and he began to calm down.

My brothers left the fire to do the farm chores as soon as the flames seemed to be under control, but suggested that I stay to help. I began to regret staying behind, though, when, as the sun was setting, the warden drafted me and Johnny Mitchell, an older boy, to stay overnight to make sure that a blaze didn't break out again. We agreed, but forgot to ask how we were to spread the alarm if we needed help. We were nearly two miles from the nearest phone, without even a bicycle.

The men left us sandwiches, drinking water, two water pumps, some rakes, and a flashlight. The longest day of the year was approaching, so it wasn't dark until very late, but as twilight faded I was wary of what looked to be a long night ahead in unfamiliar territory. The woods were still filled with smoke and

15

little fires were smoldering underground, so we were kept busy for the first few hours piling dirt over these. After it got completely dark, however, we were alarmed to see that the ground between the trees in the darkest parts of the woods was glowing with an eerie white light. We thought that fire was breaking out everywhere and were debating whether to run for help when we noticed it was the roots of the trees glowing where they had been dug up by the tractor. Johnny, who had graduated from high school, told me it was probably the phosphorus in the tree roots that was shining. He had heard that trees sometimes absorb it from the virgin soil of the woods and create a glow much like the one sailors see in the ocean. We dug up a few roots to take home in the morning, and I watched them continue to glow for several nights.

Nothing happened after that except for a few animal noises too far away to worry about, but it was impossible to sleep on the rough ground. When the sun rose we walked back to our farm, very tired, and hungry for Ma's big breakfast before Johnny caught a ride to his home with the milk truck. The warden went to the site the next day to check the damage, write a report, and pick up his equipment. Battling the fire had been hot, sweaty work, but it was an exciting welcome change from picking rocks. Even more welcome, a week later I got a check for helping out.

It was traditional to plant the vegetable garden on Memorial Day, or as close to it as weather would allow. My brother plowed the plot with a team of horses, then harrowed and smoothed it. From the time I was a young child I liked to help with the planting. I could never wait for the first sprouts, so I often dug up a few seeds after two or three days to see why they were so slow. We always planted the peas, radishes, lettuce, carrots, cabbage, turnips, cauliflower, beans, and parsnips first, all plants that could stand a light frost. The more tender pumpkins, cucumbers, and squash, as well as the tomatoes, which we started early in the house, didn't go in until later. The row of radish seed that was always part of the early planting provided quick results and were the first things we harvested. I liked to bite into the first few tasty roots, wiping off the dirt with my handkerchief or shirttail, but after other crops were ready, the radishes were forgotten and promptly went to seed.

We saved some seed from crops of the previous year for planting, and the rest we bought from the store, priced at a nickel for each fat package. Our favorites were Hawkins Seeds, which everyone in town planted because they came from Reading, Vermont. One winter we were shocked to hear from a neighbor who had visited him, that Mr. Hawkins bought nearly all his seeds from California and other faraway places, and only packed them in colorful envelopes in his barn in Reading. Since they always grew well, we kept buying them anyway, until he went out of business.

We had several other "gardens" around the farm. The "field corn" which we fed to the pigs and chickens, was sowed in a plot some distance from the sweet corn, since corn, unlike most of the garden crop, was pollinated by wind, and we didn't want the two kinds to mix because we saved the seeds. The year we grew popcorn, we had to find another distant place for that, too. We always planted the potatoes in a spot separated from the leafy vegetables so we could dose the leafy tops of the potatoes with arsenic to get rid of the striped beetles that ate them, without getting the deadly stuff on anything edible.

It was important to plant the rows of potatoes and field corn in absolutely straight lines so we could use the horse when cultivating and hilling them. We treated the corn seed with tar so that the crows that were roosting hopefully in the trees surrounding the field would not pull it up as soon as we left. In our neighborhood, having the corn "knee high by the Fourth of July" was important to every farmer's agricultural reputation.

When the weather had warmed a bit, we dug 6 or 8 holes about two feet in diameter and a foot deep, and filled them heaping full with rotted manure which we had in abundant supply. Then we piled soil over the hills and planted the squash and pumpkins in the raised beds which would warm up faster than the surrounding soil. The cucumbers, by tradition, had to go in before sunrise on the second of June. After the June full moon, we felt that frosts were over, and we could set out the tomatoes and any flowers we had started in the house.

17

Mrs. Markres, who lived a few miles away, had a small strawberry patch, and since their blooms were very sensitive to frost, she fretted endlessly during cool spring nights that she might lose her crop. "If my berries freeze up again this year," she announced on the telephone party line, "I won't go to church all summer." Since she only went two or three times a year I wasn't sure that the Lord felt greatly threatened, and my brother said that the congregation probably wouldn't much miss the dime that she had a reputation of contributing the few times she did go. "Why doesn't she just cover them up with old bedclothes and newspapers like other people, instead of putting the blame on the Almighty?" one neighbor wondered.

While we were waiting for the first vegetables, we dug the dandelion greens that sprouted everywhere. Ma washed them over and over again to get off the grit, then boiled them with a bit of salt pork. We poured vinegar over them for dinner, and everyone considered both them and rhubarb tasty spring tonics. Sometimes we also dug the Jerusalem artichokes that grew in a patch near the chicken yard. Even these rather tasteless "starvation foods", as they were called, were fresh and a welcome change from the winter food that came out of the cellar, attic, or glass jars.

Our garden was essential for our food supply and we always ate well, even during the Depression. "Boughten" food was so rare that I considered it a real treat. Store bread toasted more evenly than homemade, and made nicer-looking sandwiches, I thought, even if they didn't taste as good. Store cookies came in bulk in a wide variety, and I loved them all. And even though we caught trout and perch from our little brook in the spring and summer, store salmon was pretty tasty occasionally. We bought bananas on special occasions, and once in a while relatives from away brought us delicious blueberries, peaches, and grapes, which didn't grow on our northern farmland.

The cattle and pigs kept our table supplied with meat, milk, and butter, and our poultry furnished fowl and eggs. We ate the older birds and young roosters, usually in a chicken pie or thick gravy with biscuits for Sunday dinner. The flock kept us supplied with eggs throughout the spring, summer and fall, enough for us to use and a few dozen extra to take to the store each week to trade for the flour, coffee and white sugar we used. While we were shopping, the grocer "candled" the eggs by examining each one through a hole in a big box that had a light within. The bigger the space at the end of the egg, the older it was, he told us. "Candling" the eggs was necessary because so many farm flocks ran loose in the summer, and often laid their eggs outdoors. When the farmers found a nest with a dozen or so eggs in it, it might have already been in the warm sun for two weeks.

The local shoppers didn't buy all the eggs the farmers took to the stores, so the grocers shipped them off by train to Boston in huge crates tied with string. I wondered if the eggs from our little chicken house would appear on the table of some fine home in Boston.

Chapter 2

Fireflies and Fireworks

"Harry Sawyer don't need no firecrackers to celebrate the Fourth of July. He does it every day of the year by shootin' off his mouth." Caleb Waterhouse.

July raced by far faster than January or February. There was so much more to see and hear and taste and do. On warm summer nights in early July I lifted the screen out of my upstairs bedroom window and leaned out to watch thousands of fireflies put on their fireworks in the moist field that sloped to the brook below our house. It was like a magic show when they gathered on the screen and flashed their eerie lights across the room after I had gone to bed. Sometimes I took an empty jelly jar outdoors and caught a few to take upstairs in the jar, as a night light on my dresser.

Flickering fireflies always signaled it was time to look for ripe wild strawberries. The tiny delicacies carpeted the worn-out soils of our pastures in late June and early July. Sometimes my sister would go berrying with me, but often I was on my own. Each summer I had to hunt for them all over again since they were not always in the same places where they had grown in previous years. When I was lucky, I'd find a big patch where fat berries grew on long stems, but usually the tiny little fruits were hidden close to the ground. The discolored leaves with a reddish hue that were scattered about made the job even more challenging.

It took a long time to pick enough so that my small, metal peanut butter pail was even half full. It was tempting to eat the sweet berries as I picked them one by one, but I knew that putting them in the pail was better because then we could have shortcake for supper. Ma would remove all the tiny hulls, sweeten them with sugar, pour them over a hot biscuit cake, and top it with whipped cream, made from the cream that she had skimmed from the top of the milk that night. I thought her

21

shortcake tasted better than anything else on earth, even maple syrup. The summer I was nine, a visiting preacher in our church had said his idea of Heaven was not golden streets and pearly gates, but a place where strawberries ripened eternally. It was one of the few memorable sermons that year, and sounded like good solid theology to me.

I took advantage of the short wild strawberry season whenever I could, even if I didn't have a pail with me, and my fingers were often stained red. When I was near the vegetable garden, I picked a couple of large lettuce leaves and made a strawberry sandwich, or if I was near a marsh, I discovered that peppermint or spearmint leaves were a fine substitute for the bread, too.

When I was very young I always went barefoot while strawberrying, but one day in an unguarded moment I stepped on a wiggly snake and very nearly passed out in fright. Garter snakes frequented the warm slopes where the berries grew best and though everyone said they were harmless, I, like most country folks, was terrified of them. After that incident I always wore shoes or boots even if it was a hot day and became extremely cautious about reaching down amongst the leaves for a fat clump of berries.

Strawberry season dovetailed with the Fourth of July and we kids looked forward to that holiday as much as we did Christmas. Our anticipation had nothing to do with patriotism, but this holiday seemed designed for pure pleasure and held no obligations. We didn't have to recite 'pieces' as we did for Memorial Day or cut out turkeys as we did for Thanksgiving. There was no teacher urging us to make silly valentines, or plant a tree, as on Arbor Day. Our village didn't have a parade and the church had given up its annual community picnic and baseball game.

The local stores seldom changed their displays, even for Christmas, but in the middle of June, packages of fireworks in red, white, and blue wrappings appeared on the counters. On my rare trips to town, I looked them over with great interest, particularly coveting the rockets and pinwheels that I never had enough money for. Instead, I chose a few cents worth of sparklers and Roman candles and hoped that my brothers would bring some firecrackers to our celebration.

In the absence of commercial noisemakers, my friend Roger and I felt we had to build our own, a project my family would not have approved of, if they had been consulted. One Sunday afternoon in late June when he came to visit, we decided to build a rocket. I'd been experimenting with a recipe for gunpowder I'd found in an old book in our bookcase that called for saltpeter, sulfur, and charcoal. There was always a good supply of saltpeter and sulfur around the house for use as animal medicine and for plant diseases, so all we had to do was find some charcoal.

I remembered seeing lots of it in the pasture where someone had burned trees to clear the land, so we scooped up a full can, took it behind the barn, and got to work. It wasn't a simple job. We first pounded the charcoal into fine bits with a hammer and mixed it carefully with the saltpeter and sulfur. I'd read that if the powder mixture was packed too solid it wouldn't burn fast enough to give the missile a quick thrust, so I held a pencil in the center of a small mailing tube while Roger packed the powder mixture around it. Then we carefully removed the pencil.

We glued a pointed cardboard top on the other end, and stuffed more of our gunpowder into a drinking straw to use for the fuse, which we inserted into the hole left by the pencil. Finally, we tied a stick to the contraption, to act as a stabilizer, stuck it into some loosened earth, and tipped the pointed end toward the area of the sky where we thought Mars might be located in the daytime.

I volunteered to light the straw-fuse and Roger didn't object. He crouched behind a nearby stone wall to await the launching while I lit a match, touched it to the straw, and then ran as fast as my legs would go to join him. He had seen rockets set off at the fair and said that they always made a loud boom as they left the earth. We waited only a short time before we saw a brilliant whoosh of fire and lots of smoke, but heard no noise. Our rocket struggled three feet into the wild blue yonder before it tipped over and died in a burst of fire and a cloud of pungent smoke.

We raced to the launching pad and quickly stamped out the little grass fires before they could spread. My heart beat furiously and I hoped none of my family had seen the fire or smelled the smoke. Both of us knew that both his folks and mine had a dim view of our chemical experiments, especially if they involved fire or explosives. But I didn't give up, and managed some small successes. The closest thing to a rocket I managed that year was two firecrackers taped inside a funnel-shaped cone, one with a fuse a half inch longer than the other. The cracker that went off first shot the cone high in the air where the second one would go off with a loud bang. I also made some good sparklers by collecting iron filings from the sawhorse where my brother sharpened crosscut saws. I mixed them with melted sulfur, pasted the concoction onto a wire and lit one end. As I twirled it above my head, it produced a glorious shower of sparks.

When one of the commercial firecrackers my brothers bought didn't go off properly, which was often, we unwrapped it and looked over the Chinese newsprint it was wrapped in. Now and then we would cut a cracker in two pieces, separate them slightly, and carefully place a lighted match between them. It was fun to watch them spit at each other in a "cat and dog" fight.

The year I was 10, I was thrilled when one of my older brothers who lived in another town brought me a cap pistol and several rolls of caps. It was a very noisy Fourth that year around our place, and in the weeks that followed, at various times I became a cop, train robber, cowboy, butcher, spy, or a super detective, depending on what I was reading and whether Dick Tracy, Tom Mix, Gangbusters, or the Shadow was most appealing on the radio that week.

The holiday was never a pleasant time for my mother. She worried that a Roman candle might burn longer than it should and fall on the wooden shingles of one of our roofs, or that someone would pick up a firecracker when it hadn't gone off promptly. She was also afraid that someone would be burned by a sparkler or drop it on something explosive. Fortunately we never started any fires and none of us ever got hurt, though each year we heard of fires ignited and of people who lost their fingers, so her worrying was valid. My mother insisted, on the morning after the Fourth, that I remove any evidence of the night before, and pick up all the sparkler wires, Roman candle casings, and pieces of firecrackers strewn over the lawn.

The year I was 12, the Fourth was a real celebration. One of my brothers took my sister and me to the public beach on the lake in the village for the festivities. It was a warm evening and the beach filled quickly with many other farm families. As soon as it began to get dark, we could see displays of colorful fireworks all around the lake set off by campers from their docks or boats. The noise echoed across the water and hit the nearby hills which magnified the echoing booms. Along with many of the other kids, I took off my shoes and socks and waded out into the lake so I could see more of the lights flashing around the shore.

On the way home from the lake we saw an owl swosh low and numerous bats. Warm summer nights were busy times for bats, especially the flocks that dwelled in our various farm buildings and the attic of our house. Each evening as twilight fell and the night became darker, they whooshed from the eaves on their nightly forays to find insects and bugs. Since their radar didn't seem to distinguish a person from a bug, they swooped around anyone who happened to be outdoors. I was uncomfortable when they came too close, but my sister always became panicky, terrified that the flying rodents would get caught in her hair, as common lore had convinced her they would. They never did, as far as I knew.

I had a wonderful time throwing stones high in the air and watching the diving bats follow them to the ground, sometimes stunning themselves in their eagerness to catch any moving object. One of our cats leaped high in the air to catch them as they flew around the interior of the barn, but except for her and me, they didn't have any enemies and, like the plantain in the yard, seemed to increase in number each year. Naturalists often wrote about how valuable they were, but I never met any local people who shared that view.

Sometime during the week of the Fourth my mother's family of 10 brothers and sisters had a reunion. Some of her many relatives had deserted Vermont farms to seek better paying jobs in the foundries and machine shops of Connecticut and Massachusetts and because 250 miles was so far to travel, we saw them only on the Fourth or at a family funeral.

The reunion was always held in Vermont because many of her local kinfolk were dairy farmers, as we were, and couldn't leave the cows for a three day trip to "civilization," as our Connecticut Uncle Fritz called the Hartford area. Also, the city folks, with their small city homes and apartments, couldn't have easily entertained the crowd of 60 or so and their cars. The Vermonters suspected, too, that some of the down-country men my aunts had married liked to come north each year for the sole purpose of seeing how their less fortunate provincial in-laws were making out.

On the farms there was plenty of room for everyone to socialize and for the children to spread out and make a loud racket. I'm not sure who decided where to meet each year, but I always hoped it wouldn't be at our farm because it was more fun to go away from home. Getting to wherever we were going was always an adventure. The only paved road I'd ever seen ran through the main street of Morrisville, 25 miles away, and the 'highways' we took were rough dirt roads filled with potholes. The trip over such roads was likely to take well over an hour, even if it was not far away, making it necessary to begin getting ready for the noontime reunion as soon as morning chores were done.

On the way to Uncle Bill's and Aunt Sarah's we passed a series of clever signs advertising Burma Shave which changed each year. One set faced the traffic on the right side of the road, and another faced the left, so we enjoyed different clever sayings in each direction. Some gave driving tips: "He thought that - Proper distance was bunk - Until they pulled - Him out of - Some guy's trunk - Burma Shave." Others philosophized about romance: "He got - The ring - He got - The flat - She felt - His face - And that - Was that - Burma Shave."

The year I turned thirteen, I missed the signs because the reunion was held at our home. Preparations started early. My mother felt it necessary to clean the house from attic to cellar once again, even though spring cleaning was barely finished.

"No telling where relatives might go," we all knew. The menfolk had to work as hard as the women to neaten up outdoors, clean the barn, and figure out where to put the cars so they wouldn't block the road. We didn't have enough chairs, so it was my job to lay hardwood planks over inverted sap buckets for seats.

It was fun to watch the cars arrive, one by one, on the morning of the reunion. They were mostly Fords, Chevrolets, and Plymouths, but relatives from "away" might show up in a Buick, and one uncle even had a Terraplane. Even though it was 15 years old, he kept it so clean and polished it looked like new. Most of the Vermont folks greeted each other with friendly hellos, but some of the city women were less reserved and embraced everyone. I was very embarrassed as one plump aunt plastered a kiss on me, and I waited my chance to sneak out of sight and wipe it off.

I especially enjoyed seeing everyone unpacking food from their vehicles and wondering what they'd brought. The women headed for the kitchen, carrying big baskets and bundles and promptly busied themselves getting the meal ready, talking non-stop as they worked. By a few minutes after noon, they had spread everything out on the tables we had set up in the yard. Each Aunt brought her specialty, and I looked for some of the treats I remembered from previous reunions-the wonderful potato salad, chicken sandwiches, egg sandwiches, and sweet sticky honey, home-made from clover blossoms, that we poured over warm biscuits.

Everyone formed a line and I couldn't wait to get in it but I had been duly warned to be polite and let the grownups go first. Some of my aunts looked to me as if they could handle a lot of food, so I was somewhat nervous that the food would be gone before I reached it as I watched them fill up the plates they had brought with them. It turned out there was plenty left by the time it was my turn, enough so we each could go back for second and third helpings. Though Yankees were pretty thrifty about most things, they never liked to skimp on food.

The desserts were my favorites. Aunt Anne had brought her blueberry pie which was a rare treat, and the huge selection of mince, raisin, custard, and maple sugar pies made a   decision difficult. Someone had made a three layered checkerboard cake with thick frosting made of confectionery sugar, which got a lot of attention. Uncle Joe carved a huge watermelon he'd brought from Connecticut, the first one I'd ever seen. It looked very inviting but I wasn't sure I liked its watery consistency. Spitting the seeds around was its greatest merit, I decided.

Someone also brought small individual tubs of ice cream he had picked up at the United Farmers milk plant. We'd never had ice cream at the reunion before, and the tubs filled with half chocolate and half vanilla, which we ate with little wooden paddles were a real novelty. It was all packed in dry ice which most of us had never seen before, and we couldn't imagine how it worked. Cousin Mike dropped a piece of the ice into a glass pitcher of water, and we stood watching it, fascinated as the water 'boiled' furiously for a long time. Everyone who came by stuck their fingers in it to see if it was hot.

Ma's sisters were all large women, like she was, and her brothers were just the opposite, tall and skinny. But they all had in common the gift of being relaxed conversationalists and seemed able to talk and listen to each other at the same time, like some of the Italian granite workers in the next town. The older women, after dinner and cleaning up, sat talking in the living room, while the older men gathered in chairs on the lawn, lit up their pipes, and reminisced about their growing up. The younger men wandered off to look over and compare each other's cars. The farmers discussed cows, grains, fertilizer, and horses, and walked around to inspect our animals and vegetable garden, probably comparing every detail to their own. Since our farm was in the north and high in the Green Mountains, summer always arrived there much later than in the lowlands where most of our kinfolks lived. Consequently we had to listen to a lot of comments about our tardy season. The Massachusetts folks invariably pointed out that they had been eating peas for three weeks, while ours were only beginning to blossom. The Connecticut kin then remarked that they were already dining on fresh tomatoes, as they looked over our small growing plants. Everyone seemed to enjoy the good-natured kidding, but it seemed to me they were implying that the retarded summer was somehow our fault, either for electing to stay in the North or being negligent in our work and planning. I proudly pointed out that we beat all of them with the first snowflakes, but clearly none of them were envious.

I went off to join a group of the school-age boys and girls who had gathered for a game of croquet in back of the house where the hay was still short. Croquet wasn't easy on our hilly yard, and the city cousins complained that whenever they hit a ball it always rolled too far. When we tired of croquet, some of us went to the woods beside the brook to play hide and seek. I thought we should throw rocks in the brook, but they wanted to do something more exciting. So we went to the barn, which was usually a good place to play but not much fun at this time of year because we hadn't started haying yet and couldn't climb up on the high beams and jump into the fresh, loose hay. We didn't have a big empty silo, either, as some of my uncles did, to yell in and listen to the echoes. That day we mostly just ran around in the empty hay lofts.

None of us ever got seriously hurt at these events despite the temptations and the active cast of characters, but my little niece got a bloody nose that year. She was running around the house in a spirited game of anti-over and collided head-on around a corner with a small chunky cousin running from the other direction. Several minor scratches resulted, from encounters with unfamiliar barbed wire, and when one of the neatly dressed little girls stepped into some of the fresh cow manure scattered around the pastures she cried openly while the boys howled with laughter.

Billy, one of my city cousins, thought it would be fun to hop on the back of our rake horse, Molly, who was in a nearby pasture that afternoon. He jumped from a rock, but Molly knew what was happening and wasn't interested in giving rides. She moved quickly, and Billy fell flat in some mud and started crying. Fortunately, he wasn't hurt, and his parents barely took notice. Everyone seemed to feel that minor bruises were normal for a reunion and my uncles and aunts seemed rather oblivious to whatever their offspring were doing. They appeared not to be concerned even when their children tried to ride our two-wheeled rake down the hill, or when a noisy duel with pitchforks erupted.

My mother, however, was capable of worrying enough for all of them, and was very much afraid that someone would get hurt at our place. She became visibly upset when she saw several cousins spread out, like monkeys, throughout the huge maple tree in our yard that she and my father had planted when they were married, the one tree her own children had always been strictly forbidden to climb. She made no comments until after everyone had left, but I saw her carefully inspecting the tree for any possible damage. Since I had a precedent, however, after the reunion I, too, began climbing the mammoth tree occasionally to enjoy the view from the top. I always chose the time very carefully, when Ma was busy and out of sight.

Meeting my city cousins always reminded me that my life was quite different from theirs. They talked about going to the circus, baseball games, carnivals, and discussed new movies they had seen. I knew that those movies wouldn't reach a theater near us for at least another year, and even then I wouldn't be able to go. They didn't seem at all envious of the fishing, hunting, horseback riding and swimming we had on our farm. I tried not to be envious, but deep down I felt that a life that included glamorous movie stars, big bands, and the well-known sports figures who occasionally visited their cities, might be more exciting than catching fireflies, listening to screech owls, and hunting woodchucks.

When I got tired of chasing around with the kids, I stopped to listen to some of the grownups. Most of their conversation involved people I had never heard of, but I enjoyed listening to Uncle Robert, who was a patrol officer on the Canadian Border just a few miles to our north. A few of us talked him into showing us his big Smith and Wesson revolver and the .45 caliber cartridges in the half moon clip in the cylinder. He kept this intriguing object in his car which he carefully locked, just in case it proved too tempting to us. Once more, as at every reunion, we asked him about chasing liquor smugglers during the 20s, and his adventures with cattle dealers who drove large herds of cows through the woods from one country to the other during the night. He told us that many people bought farms that were partly in each country just for smuggling purposes, and most quickly became very rich.

Two of my other uncles, Uncle Pete and Uncle Ned, had both left New England to seek their fortunes in the early 1900's in Colorado where they had worked on a ranch. I sought them out, as I always did at reunions because I'd been steeped in Western lore from reading dime novels and listening to Tom Mix radio shows and was sure that they must have been involved with countless cowboys, Indians, train robbers, and horse thief hangings.

Each reunion I hoped that they might remember something I hadn't already heard about their adventures, but unfortunately, they must have been in a dull part of the West. On their ranch, everyone seemed to work as hard as we did on the farm, with no time for any excitement. Not once did they see a shootout in the OK corral or a quick draw outside the Longbranch on Main Street at high noon. They didn't sing cowboy songs in the bunkhouse or ride wild bulls for the fun of it. The most excitement they could recall was when a few drunks got into a fist fight in town on Saturday night. Since that was a normal occurrence in the mill town next to ours every weekend, I was very disappointed. They also said that the only sixguns they ever saw were those the photographers provided young cowhands to wear for the pictures they sent back home. I mentioned once to my classmates that I had two uncles who had been cowboys, but then wished I hadn't when they wanted to know all about their adventures.

The party started to break up soon after mid-afternoon, since the farm families had to get home in time to do evening chores. Aunt Bessie's family, from Connecticut, spent the night with Uncle Donald and Aunt Sophie before making the long trip south. Their son told me later that Aunt Bessie liked to relive her younger days on a Spartan farm and remembered well the privy, the lack of closets, and other such deprivations. But her urban-bred husband and children failed to find much joy living with no electricity or running hot water. Uncle Donald said later, "The kids made so much racket that night that the cows didn't give much milk."

The day after the reunion that year we began haying, and I mulled over my city cousins and wondered what it would be like to live the way they did without having to worry about haying or other farm chores. As I helped to put the harnesses on the big, smelly horses, I imagined what it would be like to have a truck and tractor and not deal with horses.

Each year there were a few auctions in our town in early summer and if they were nearby, occasionally my brothers went. Auctions were social gatherings that farmers, and sometimes their wives, could attend without feeling guilty about taking a day off, since they might be able to pick up a useful item or two. I didn't enjoy going to auctions and would have preferred to go to the brook to play on a day off, but when our neighbor Stan Wakeman sold out, it seemed as if everyone *had* to attend. Auctions usually meant a final chapter in someone's life, so they were often sad occasions. It might be a sellout of farm animals and machinery due to a bank foreclosure, or it might be a disposal of everything, including household goods, to settle an estate. In the case of Stan, his wife had died and he decided to give up farming and move into a small house in another town. The sale would enable him to get rid of the accumulations of a lifetime and, hopefully, make a little money to live on.

Most folks got to the auction as early as possible so they could look things over. His farm machinery was sparkling with its first-ever washing, other than in a heavy rain. The pieces that were in terribly bad shape were conveniently dirty and covered with manure to hide years of wear, as the auctioneer had advised Stan. Everyone knew when he had bought each wagon and plow, in any case, and probably how much he had paid for them, so they weren't easily fooled.

His three work horses got their teeth looked at so often before the bidding started, my brother said he was surprised they didn't smile when anyone came near them. Checking the horse's mouth was necessary to indicate the animal's age and general health, everyone said, but I thought it was like kicking tires on a used car-more a tradition than an exercise of much value. The cows had milk dripping from their udders and I overheard someone say that Stan had obviously milked them soon after midnight so they would look very productive at the time of the sale.

I was glad to see some other kids there. A few of the older boys were looking ahead to stocking the farms they themselves would own some day, but we younger ones were just enjoying the outing. Some were playing with the equipment, hopping on the horses, or climbing up and sitting in the high open windows of the barn. Since most men owned no casual clothes, only Sunday best and work duds, they wore bib overalls, baggy denim frocks, and few had bothered to shave for the occasion. The women were sporting well starched aprons and most wore their Sunday hats.

There were no seats, but a few men and boys perched on wagons or hung out of the open barn windows where they could get a good view. No one served lunch at these auctions, but most of the crowd stayed until the sale ended in mid-afternoon. The auctioneer was a short, thin man wearing a leather vest and a black derby hat, and I thought he should have been acting on a stage, he was so skilled as an entertainer. He was also adept at getting the highest possible bids from the crowd. "I'll take your bids every way you give them," he announced early. "Wave, nod, or yell, but don't wink. I sold an ox yoke to a woman once, who denied even making a bid. 'You winked at me, didn't you?' I accused. 'Well, you winked first, you old fool,' she said."

Two men who came with the auctioneer led the animals one by one into a sort of ring formed by the crowd and paraded them around as Stan described each one. Machinery was next on the agenda, and the crowd moved to the area where it was displayed. The household and personal goods went on the block last. The thrifty Yankee farmers often fell under the auctioneer's spell and quickly bid a quarter or so on a heap of rusty stovepipe or a box of crooked nails and bolts. The people who were able to stay until the rest had run out of money got the best bargains, but the auctioneer had cleverly sold the good stuff first. He offered most of the junk in lots along with something fairly desirable, just to get rid of it. I saw Ed Cristie carry off some rotten harnesses because a good hog box was included, and Jack Forge latched onto two worn-out whiffletrees so he could get the coil of copper tubing he had come for. I enjoyed watching Freddy Fair, a man, my brother said was a regular at every auction. Freddy bid on everything that came up, but never bought a thing. I kept hoping he would get caught, but he apparently was very good at his hobby.

Even at my age, I felt sad to see the personal collections of the Wakemans' lifetime brought out and sold to the highest bidder. Stan disappeared after the livestock and machinery were sold, not wanting to see their household furniture, children's toys, and personal possessions drift away. Even though everyone was trying to have fun, times were hard, and many were probably thinking that some day an event like this would be their own fate.

Chapter 3

One Good Season

"There ain't but two decent months in Vermont, and then, by gory, you hafta hay." Skinny Logan.

Haying began right after the Fourth of July. The farmers in our neighborhood believed that anyone who started earlier was sure to suffer all the storms of late June in addition to those following the holiday which the oldtimers said were caused by all the noise and smoke of gunpowder burning. My mother told me that my grandfather and other Civil War veterans claimed it always rained hard after a big battle. Things didn't always work out the way the older residents promised, of course, but everyone remembered only the times they did.

The cutting, drying, and storing of hay to feed the cattle and horses for the long winter ahead dominated our summer. Though our city cousins and summer visitors were thrilled with the process and talked about the sweet scent of hay drying in the fields and happy rides on high loads of loose fluffy hay, in my opinion there was good reason for the expression "dull as hay." I didn't particularly like its smell and preferred to walk behind the loads when we took it to the barn. The dry hay was itchy and prickly on my bare legs and through my thin summer clothes, and I couldn't find any pleasure in the way the chaff stuck to the bare skin of overheated, sticky human bodies and sweaty horses. I disliked the tense, wild rush to get in a load of hay before an approaching thunder shower, and I couldn't wait to get out of the hot barn where we had to tuck one load after another into the dark back corners and crevices.

There didn't seem to be any shortcuts to haying, though I always tried to find some way to make it go faster. My brothers always cut the hay with a mower, a two-wheeled machine with a seat, pulled by two horses. It had a sickle bar that stuck out on the right side, and the cutting sections, powered by the wheels, moved back and forth along it to chop off the standing hay.

Although my ancestors had spent several generations splitting the rocks left behind by the latest glacier for their stone walls and building foundations, plenty were left in every field. A few farmers in our neighborhood avoided spreading manure near the rocks in the hayfields so the hay would be thin there and they could spot them more easily, but my brothers, like most Yankees, wanted every spear they could get. They always banged up the mower each year as they slammed into rocks.

Gathering each possible spear of hay, in the Yankee tradition of "Waste Not, Want Not", meant that we had to scythe wherever the mower couldn't go-in corners, close to the fences, and all the rocky roadsides. It was important to use the scythe, also, for the sake of neatness, so the neighbors wouldn't talk about our slovenly ways. Time and labor seemed to be the only commodities good Yankees were allowed to waste.

As the youngest member of my family, I was assigned several duties not directly connected with cutting the hay. Each day, before my brothers mowed, I had to round up our cats so they wouldn't get cut. It took a long time because it was difficult to catch them all and carry them to our shop, the only building that was cat-tight except the house. The cats loved to hunt in the hayfields which were full of mice, and even though the mower made a lot of noise, instead of running away the cats tended to crouch down and hide, hoping not to be seen.

My family felt it was most humane, if a cat had been injured by the mower, to destroy it promptly. Other neighbors felt differently, and several three-legged cats roamed around some farms. It was always sad to lose one of my favorite pets, so I tried very hard to locate them all whenever any cutting was planned near the farm buildings.

One year my brother mowed into a tiny fawn that its mother had parked in a field of tall hay during the day while she went off in search of food. We were all very upset, because we knew that the distressed mother would spend many days searching for her baby. Fortunately that kind of thing didn't happen often because deer were so scarce in our neighborhood.

Another of my jobs, one I considered boring and unproductive, was to turn the grindstone while someone sharpened the scythes and the cutter bars for the mowing machine. The men could keep their scythes sharp for a time with a whetstone before they needed grinding, but the cutter bars had to be removed from the machine frequently for sharpening. Each of the small blades, called sections, had to be held against the grindstone on both sides, and it seemed to take hours. As I sat on a bucket cranking the spinning stone, I tried to keep my mind on something more interesting, such as what I would do on Sunday afternoon.

One day Mr. Rogers stopped by when I was cranking and told us that his hired man, who would never have been electrocuted for his brains, kept turning the stone even while his boss was changing scythes. "'You don't need to crank it when I ain't sharpening', Joe, I told him," Rogers said. "But he said he thought it wouldn't do no hurt to get a few turns ahead."

The mowing season sometimes brought unexpected entertainment as well as little disasters. Our neighbor John Rice always talked to himself while he worked, and when he was mowing he had to talk very loud to be able to hear himself above the noisy machine. If the wind was right, we picked up some revealing monologues that included John's somewhat prejudiced opinions about the neighborhood, the Democrats, his wife, and the world in general. It was hard to believe he was alone and not carrying on a heated argument with a large crowd. We all enjoyed those little episodes, and they taught me to never talk to myself out loud, even if I thought I was alone.

Since the horse rake, like the mowing machine, couldn't get close to the walls, fences, and big rocks where the hay had been scythed, another of my jobs was to rake out those spots with a long-handled wooden rake and move the hay to a position where the mechanical rake could reach it. Since the ground was always rough in those spots, I had to be careful not to break the wooden teeth out of the big rake on the rough terrain. From experience, I had discovered that my brothers didn't much enjoy whittling out replacements for the teeth on a busy day.

One of the potential hazards of raking by hand was getting into the nests of yellow hornets that often appeared in the ground and on bushes around the edge of a hayfield. More than once I was grateful that we lived far away from other people when I had to take off my pants in record time as the wicked little stingers moved up my legs. One day they were so persistent that I had to run and plunge into the brook that bordered the hayfield to escape their fury.

I was instructed at an early age that the best remedy for a hornet or bee sting was to carefully dig out the stinger and quickly plaster the wound either with mud or the juice of plantain weed. But nobody explained how to find mud in a hayfield on a hot July day, and plantain seemed to grow only on our well-traveled lawn. Consequently, I often had painful swellings on various parts of my body during the summer months. I never got much sympathy from members of my family, because they often had a lump or two of their own.

Hornets were hazardous to the horses, too, and if a swarm attacked, it usually resulted in a runaway team, an exciting and dangerous event. One of my brothers was raking with a horse rake one day when the horses bolted after hitting a nest. He was unable to stop them and they all collided with a large butternut tree that grew in the middle of the field. He was shaken, but emerged better than the rake, which needed major repairs.

All of us became very thirsty as we labored in the hot sun, so we stopped for water after unloading each load of hay in the barn, and if we were turning or "cocking" hay, I was usually sent to the house for a two quart glass jar of fresh, cold, spring water. Like most other local farmers, at least once or twice each year we had the traditional haying drink of switchel which reputedly could quench thirst better than anything else. People disagreed on the precise recipe, but it was usually a combination of vinegar, water, sugar, molasses, ginger, and sometimes a little baking soda which would react with the vinegar and produce a fizz. Some farm families, we heard, even added oatmeal to the concoction. No matter how my mother made it, I never found it had any redeeming qualities and preferred to drink water.

Far better than switchel, in my opinion, was the batch of root beer my mother made at least once each summer. She started it in a big kettle with a small bottle of root beer extract from the store to which she added five gallons of water, some yeast, and a mess of sugar. After letting it set in the warm pantry for a day or so, she poured it into bottles and canning jars and set them in a warm place for a few days where it could "work." If it got too warm, as it usually did, it popped a few corks from the bottles and squirted over the room. We tried to remember to move it into the cool cellar after we thought it had "worked" enough, but often forgot and had to clean up the sticky mess. It was worth all the trouble, though. With a little ice added, the root beer tasted terrific on a hot, sweaty day.

After the mown hay had dried a bit on one side, we turned it over by hand with 3-tined pitchforks so it could dry faster. Then my brother or sister raked it with a dump rake, a contraption about 10 feet wide with two large wheels and a series of curved tines, that was pulled by a single horse. The tines could be raised with a foot pedal when they were full of hay, which allowed it to be bunched together in rows. The rows made it easier for us to form the little round heaps, called tumbles, that we could later pick up with hand forks and toss on the hay wagon.

If the weather looked as if rain might fall before we could get all the mown hay in the barn, we sometimes piled two tumbles together, one on top of another, in what everyone called a "cock". The theory was that haycocks would shed the rain and dry out faster than tumbles after the sun came out. I always felt that piling up haycocks was just one more way Yankee farmers devised to keep busy.

Bad weather was unquestionably the biggest obstacle to getting the haying done, and we always tried to find out from the radio in advance what the upcoming weather might be. Until we got electricity, we used a battery radio that needed three different batteries. We listened sparingly because the large glass tubes inside used a lot of power which wore out the batteries quickly. The dozen or so tubes didn't last long either, so running the radio, like using an automobile, was a luxury.

When electricity finally reached our neighborhood, we bought an electric radio, and because we lived a long distance from any radio station, we needed an antenna wire that stretched all the way from our house to a back shed. Whenever there was a thunderstorm threatening, one of us carefully unhooked the antenna so if lightning struck nearby, it wouldn't come into the house on the wire and wreck the radio. We had learned about this threat from our neighbors, the Reynolds. One day when they returned home after a storm, they found that lightning had blown their brand new Philco all over the living room.

Unfortunately, because our radio weather reports originated in Albany, Boston, or Montreal, the forecasts were far from reliable for our area. Meteorologists 200 miles away usually had no idea what was going on in the mountains of northern Vermont, and Aunt Sal's rheumatism or Hiram Potter's war wound were far better indicators. Nevertheless, we listened every day when the Old Squire, owner of our local station, dutifully read them. From experience, he wisely added, "I know not what the truth may be, but tell the tale as 'twas told to me."

To predict the weather for our neighborhood, we could more accurately depend on signs in the sky and the actions of the animals and birds. Cows lying down in the pasture during the day and swallows gathered in groups on the telephone wires indicated it might not be a good idea to mow down too much hay. We knew that it was not a good idea to mow either, if there was a red sunrise, a strong east wind, or we could hear the whistle of the train down in the valley. A circle around the sun or moon, a mackerel sky, or high horsetail clouds indicated we had maybe a couple of days before the next storm. High flying birds, red sunsets, a north wind, or smoke rising high in the air gave us more confidence, although, like radio forecasts, they were not always reliable predictors, either.

Rains delayed haying and made it harder, but occasionally weather events on perfectly beautiful days ruined our work. Most surprising were the little whirlwinds people called 'dust devils' that appeared out of nowhere. They could mess up an entire day's work in only a few seconds. We called them little tornados because they acted so much like the real thing. In the middle of a bright sunny afternoon they would arrive with no warning and, for some unknown reason, usually hit just after we had finished bunching a field of hay into neat tumbles. As we stood by and watched, a small whirlwind would start at the edge of a field and swirl rapidly across the field, increasing in strength as it moved.

It lifted each hay tumble in its path high into the air, shredded it, and scattered it over a wide area, making it look as if it had never been raked. Once, as we watched helplessly, a 'devil' actually turned around and made another pass, messing up the few hay piles it had missed the first time around. I thought the whirlwinds were spectacular, even if they obliterated a day's work and we had to do it over, but I was always concerned that they might turn into a real tornado, pick up the house, a few cows, and spin us around a few times before dropping each one, who knows where, as I had read in The Wizard of Oz.

Our neighbors seemed to have more exciting winds than we did, or perhaps they were just better storytellers. Jack Rogers claimed he had seen a whirlwind pick up a large hay cock, lift it intact over his big barn, and deposit it on the back porch of the house. Little Tommy Tobias told me that when his family was watching their work disappear into the air one day, his grandmother ran and sat on a hay tumble. "It was the only one left intact after things calmed down," he said. "If the rest of us had acted as quickly as she did, we could have saved five more."

Forking hay into tumbles was an art I had some trouble learning. The trick was to pick up a long wad of hay, twist it into a circle, and step on part of it, winding it up on top which made a tight little ball about thirty inches in diameter. The resulting tumble made a compact forkful that was the right size to pick up and throw up onto the hay wagon. After I had mastered the skill, three of us working together could create several hundred tumbles in only a few hours.

After the tumbling was finished, we pitched each one with a hayfork onto the hay wagon, a flat wooden rack with no sides which was set on a four wheeled frame and pulled by a two horse team. One man stayed on the wagon to load the hay and drive the horses, although after years of training they knew pretty much what to do by themselves. Pitching the hay tumbles took more muscle than skill, but loading required real expertise so the hay could be quickly unloaded, but still stay intact on the wagon during the bumpy ride to the barn.

When the hay was as piled as high as we could reach, or as heavy as the horses could pull, it was time to head for the barn.

Sometimes summer kids-boys and girls who vacationed at the lake in town-came to visit me during haying and liked to ride on top of the load of hay as it was going to the barn. We always had to yell at them to duck their heads before the wagon reached the entrance because the load reached nearly to the top of the doorway and the horses needed to run quickly to get the heavy load up the barn 'bridge', as the ramp was called. Many barns had a long ramp, usually called a 'high drive', so the farmers could toss the hay off rapidly into deep bays on either side of the barn. The cattle stable in our barn was located beneath the hay storage, however, so most of the hay had to be forked up into high piles called hay mows (rhymes with cows), which was heavy work.

It wasn't until a few years later that our farm became a bit more modern. We still didn't have a tractor, but when I was thirteen we acquired a hay loader, an upright machine that hitched onto the back of the hay wagon and automatically threw hay up onto the rack. The hay piled up so fast there was no time to bunch it up properly for easy unloading, so we got a new mechanical hay fork in the barn for that purpose. It operated by electricity and resembled two huge ice tongs. When the fork was lowered, the tongs grabbed a big wad of hay and pulled it up to the high ridge of the barn where it latched itself onto a track that ran the length of the barn. When the wad of hay reached the spot where we wanted it, someone pulled a rope and the fork opened, letting the hay fall. Then the fork returned for another load.

Both the loader and fork speeded up haying and saved us a lot of heavy work, but it wasn't a perfect solution because the fork deposited the hay in a tangled mess in the middle of the barn, and we had to pull it to the sides, and layer it out. It was not only difficult to pull apart when we initially spread it around the hay loft, but it was also a chore to pull it apart a second time when we fed it to the cattle during the winter.

The barn swallows that built nests inside our barn loft each summer loved the contrivance, and dozens of them waited patiently for every load of hay to arrive. As soon as the fork began to move the length of the long barn, they landed on the rope that pulled it, rode to the end, and, when the hay dropped, flew off. Then, when the fork was brought back to pick up another load, they all jumped back on the rope and hitched another ride all the way back to the door of the barn. Of all the birds that visited us during the summer, swallows undoubtedly had the most fun. After they raised their one and only brood they took the rest of the summer off, and when they were not riding on our hay fork, they spent their time flying high in the sky, perching on telephone wires, watching people, and swooping at our cats. I thought they were much smarter than robins and other birds who felt it necessary to promptly produce and feed another family immediately after the first fledglings had left the nest. I wondered if they raised two more broods during their winter holiday in the South.

It took us most of the summer to cut, dry, and store the first crop of hay. In the meantime a second crop was growing in the fields we had cut first, and as soon as we finished the first cutting we had to begin harvesting the next. The second crop, called rowen like the British tree, was shorter and thicker than the first, and it took longer to dry. One day a salesman who obviously had never lived in the country, asked my mother what kind of crop rowen might be. He said everybody he was looking for that morning seemed to be out harvesting it.

As soon as the hay had settled a little and there was space at the top of the hay mows, it was time to cut the oats and tuck them in there. By that time, I was back in school and could help out only on evenings and Saturdays. Many of my schoolmates were working on their farms, too, whenever they were not in school, and we found it difficult not to envy the fun the village kids were having playing ball, going hunting, or just hanging around.

Although farm life often seemed all work and no play to me, there were diversions that the village kids didn't have. One Saturday night in August that summer, Bill and Andy, two brothers from Boston who were vacationing in town came to visit us. They were about my age and I'd met them when visiting my sister who worked at the lake. They were fascinated by everything in the country, and that night we decided to sleep overnight in the loose hay in the barn, a novel experience both for them and me. We didn't get to sleep very early, because there was a lot to talk about, and I learned a lot about their life in the city that night. We woke up early, just as the sun was rising and its rays shone through the high window of the barn. At Bill and Andy's suggestion, we climbed up to the high beams and somersaulted down into the fluffy hay. I was a bit wary at first because I had been warned that broken necks could result from such "foolishness", but soon discovered it was great fun. We had to do all this early before anyone else woke up, because my family did not believe in such horseplay, especially on a Sunday morning. Besides, the boys had to bike back to the lake early, and I had to round up the cows.

Later in the month, Bill thought it would be fun to sleep outdoors in the field, as he'd done the year before when his family had vacationed in Switzerland. So, although my family thought we were crazy to choose the hard ground over soft beds, we bedded down on piles of hay in our back field. It was a beautiful night with a crescent moon that sank early, leaving a sky full of brilliant stars. An added bonus was several shooting stars and even some Northern Lights which, though they weren't too brilliant, were the first my friends had ever seen. The night seemed more exciting and scary than the overnight we'd spent in the barn because we heard owls hoot, a bobcat scream, and other noises we couldn't identify. Bill, the older of the two brothers, had brought along a big hunting knife, so we felt protected, even though we weren't sure how it might help if we were attacked by a bear while we slept.

In the morning our clothes were soaked with dew and we got our feet damp walking back to the house in the wet grass. We all drank a cup of hot cocoa and ate some of my mother's fresh graham rolls before Bill and Andy left for home and I had to attend to my barn duties. We all agreed it ought to be a regular summer event.

Our barn lacked the enormous cupola that distinguished the top of many other barns in our town. I never heard of a practical need for such a big structure perched on top of a building, but some large barns had two. Certainly nothing that large was necessary for ventilation, so it must have been built for appearance's sake, or to proclaim to all that the farmer could afford it. From time to time I visited a school friend whose family had one of these fascinating structures. On one Sunday afternoon when the grownups were busy elsewhere, we climbed up a long, rickety ladder in the dark through a maze of cobwebs to a catwalk that was equally shaky, then proceeded cautiously into the little penthouse perched high on the barn roof. Here we peered through the shutters at spectacular views in four directions. The countryside was very open, with little woodland, so we could see distant mountains and many other farms surrounded by cattle, patches of woods, and ponds. At the Reynolds farm a group of tourists was having a picnic beside the road, and in another direction, a farmer was having a rough time rounding up his pigs which had broken loose. I had always envied the men who flew little planes over our farm occasionally, and as I peered out those shutters I felt as if I were flying, too.

Because our family was large enough to handle all our own work, like most farm families, we seldom hired any help. Farmers who didn't have several sons often kept a hired man or two, however, and many of these were interesting characters. The hired help was of several types: year-round workers who usually lived with the family; part-time workers, men or boys who weren't needed to work full-time on their own family farm: and, in the summer, school boys and the teenage sons of campers at the lake who felt their sons should have the experience of working on a farm. For some young men, "hiring out" for a few years was a good way to leave home early, make a bit of money, and then buy their own farm. Sometimes they married one of their bosses' daughters and took over the farm after her father retired.

Some farm hands were men mentally unable to make it on their own, and after they had reached manhood, their families sent them out to work, often for little more than their room and board. Most remained single all their lives, and the arrangement they had with their employers was often ideal because they needed someone to manage their lives, and the farmers needed their inexpensive help.

When a farmer died before his time, it wasn't unusual for the hired man to stay on and carry on the operation with the widow. Sometimes he even married her. The same thing happened when hired girls stayed with the same family for years. They, too, occasionally married their employer if his wife went to her glory early.

Some hired men felt inferior, so they acted tough when they went to town on Saturday night to play pool, pinball machines, juke boxes, or simply hang out. They wore cowboy jeans and wide belts with colored stones imbedded in them, and they would often sit in a chair facing its back. Most tried to smoke their Camels like the "He Men" in the movies, and enjoyed bragging about their mythical female conquests. Those who could drive, occasionally borrowed their bosses' car for a night out, and a few owned ancient Indian or Harley motorcycles or noisy old cars. The rest either rode with friends, drove a horse, used a bicycle, or walked.

We had to hire a man for a few weeks when I was ten, after one of my brothers had broken his leg working in the woods. Earl was a local man, about 60 years old, with a stubble of a beard. He usually worked in the sawmill, but had been laid off for awhile so he was available. I didn't like the fact that he had to sleep in a bed in my room, but soon found it could be amusing. In the daytime Earl was grumpy and paid no attention to me, but he talked freely in his sleep and I found I could ask him all kinds of questions which he would willingly but unknowingly answer. Prompted by my questions, he discussed his ex-wife freely and how their separation came about. In the daytime, I never dared mention our nighttime conversations to him, or to tell anyone else what I had found out.

The farmers who kept hired men in their homes had to overlook a lot of their habits in exchange for reliable help. John Farnham, a church deacon, seldom mentioned his hired man's occasional drunken weekends, or that he occasionally had to lend him some money to get him out of trouble. Bill, the Hawleys' farmhand, wore long, red underwear and high rubber boots winter and summer. He never removed his boots on entering anyone's house, and Russ Hawley said he even wore them upstairs at night. "But I don't think he sleeps with them on, though" he said.

One story, probably apocryphal, made the rounds regularly about a man who worked for a farmer who couldn't afford to pay him, but instead kept giving him a share of the farm each year. After about six years, the hired man would own the farm, and the former owner had to work for him for no pay for another specified period. The farm ownership supposedly went back and forth like this until one of them died. Of course, a Yankee never actually worked for another person. He "helped out around the place," just as he was never sick but only 'under the weather' for a few days. I never met a man who'd been lost in the woods during hunting season, either. He just got a "little turned around" for several hours, sometimes getting home long after dark.

Not all hired help moved in permanently with a family. Some restless laborers planned to stay a few years at one place and then move on, often to another town. Some farm families moved every few years, too, although most of our neighbors seemed to plan on living at the same place for at least a couple of generations. One year a new family with six children moved into our neighborhood. One of their boys, Buster, was about my age, and had a face full of freckles and the most brilliant red hair I had ever seen. One day he asked me where I was born, and when I said it was where we lived now he seemed shocked. He was only 10 and had already lived in six different towns. He was even more surprised when I told him that my father and grandfather had been born in the same house I lived in. A year later, after Buster and I had become good friends, his folks moved once more and I never saw him again.

In early summer the whitewash man always appeared. Our milk went to Boston, and the Massachusetts Milk Board had decreed, for sanitary reasons, that each barn and milkroom where their milk originated had to be whitewashed every summer. It was not something we could easily do ourselves, and the board was so fussy they wouldn't have approved a homemade job anyway. I never thought it made anything more hygienic, but it did make the barn a lot lighter. The stuff took weeks to dry on the walls and stuck to us every time we went near it, but on our skin the hardening seemed to take effect immediately.

Everyone hated whitewash day. The white man, as we called him, arrived in a truck carrying several bags of white lime, a pump, and a tank of water. He stopped frequently to refill the tank in the little brooks he passed by, coloring the water considerably in the process. We were never quite sure when he might appear, although we usually were alerted when he was in the neighborhood either by hearing it on the party line, or when a few flies covered with whitewash from other barns appeared in our barn. Then we knew it was time to move everything outside that we didn't want sprayed. Whenever he surprised us, he whitewashed the windows, milk cans, baby calves, sacks of grain, and anything else that was in the barn. He must have been paid by the job because he was always in a great hurry.

I liked to watch the job from a safe distance because the spray spread wildly. Not only was his entire truck white, but the man himself was so covered from top to bottom that I wondered if we would have noticed him at all in the winter. We speculated about whether he cleaned up at night or if he even bothered. Because the job never offered a good opportunity for conversation, no one wanted to get very close to him, so we never found out anything about our anonymous white person, and we never heard what he did the rest of the year. The fee for his services was always deducted from our milk check.

Although haying dominated our summer days between morning and evening chores, other necessary duties had to be crowded into the schedule, including the eternal repairing and sharpening necessary on a farm and the cultivating and hilling up of corn and potatoes. About mid-July we began our annual battle with the potato bugs. Since we didn't own a sprayer, we used a sprinkling can to apply a toxic mixture of arsenic of lead and water over the plants. One year we planted the potatoes at the far end of one of our fields, hoping the bugs wouldn't find them, but the pests must have had a lot of scouts. As soon as the first leaves formed, they began multiplying and chewing.

Another summer job was firewood. We moved the wood we had cut during the winter into the woodshed attached to our house, and piled the long pieces of wood cut from tree limbs in the sugarhouse to prepare for boiling maple syrup the following spring. Both activities were hard jobs on hot days. It was traditional to split all the stove wood when we sawed it during the winter, though I felt we should pile the big chunks and split them later, as we used them, so there wouldn't be as many pieces of wood to handle so many times. But my family insisted that wood dried better in small chunks, and I learned early that none of my ideas would change any long-standing tradition.

A great deal of Ma's work throughout haying season and the rest of the summer revolved around food. Not only did she have to prepare three big meals each day and clean up after them, but in the summer it was necessary to can the vegetables and fruits and to make pickles, jellies and jams for winter. Ma's first job each day was breakfast. We always ate after milking, but before cleaning the barn. The menu seldom varied. It was always oatmeal with maple syrup, fresh graham rolls, doughnuts, milk, coffee, and sometimes she also fried some of the potato left over from supper. Noon dinners were large, too, usually with beef or pork, potatoes and other vegetables, doughnuts, bread or rolls, milk, and, always, pie she'd made that morning. Supper, at five o'clock before milking, included more potatoes, meat or eggs, applesauce or other fruit sauce, maple syrup, bread, cookies, and a freshly made cake. If we were hungry during the day, filled cookies, doughnuts, bread, and milk were always available, and we all knew where they were. None of us ever thought about spoiling our appetite or the possibility of gaining weight. We didn't do either.

Much of Ma's work took place in the kitchen next to our cookstove which had to be kept very hot all summer not only for cooking and baking, but also for heating the water needed for washing hands, dishes, clothes, and the milk pails needed in the barn. The stove also made our toast, warmed the flatirons, and dried wet clothes and apple slices strung on a string. On the hot, sticky summer days in the 1930s, before meals Ma often threw a pail of cold spring water on the large block of granite that was our doorstep, to cool off the house a bit while we ate.

Summers were often extremely hot in the thirties and not only were the days "sticky" but so were the nights. The upstairs rooms in our farmhouse, where we slept, seemed particularly blistering and the temperature would become bearable only after a hard thundershower, and then, only temporarily. Ma invariably woke up everyone in the house when a thunderstorm threatened in the night and insisted we get completely dressed, even when it wasn't nearby. She had good reason, since many frightening stories circulated about houses and barns being struck by lightning, and animals and people getting killed. During one frightening storm a ball of lightning went across the kitchen somewhere between the water pipe and the stove.

It was difficult, after a long day in the fields, to get up and sit around sleepily for an hour or more as thunder boomed around us and non-stop lightning flashed. Ma insisted we follow all the safety rules and stay out of any draft and away from windows, telephone, and all the plumbing and electric outlets. That meant we couldn't sit in the kitchen, so we gathered around the dining room. When a storm finally trailed off in the East, I hoped, often in vain, that there wouldn't be another following it that night.

The hot summer days and nights would make our milk sour quickly, so we needed to keep it cool until the milk truck picked it up early each morning. Until the power line was extended to our neighborhood and we got a mechanical milk cooler, we cooled it with the ice we had cut every winter on the pond a mile away in the woods behind our house. We had an insulated tank half full of water that we would drop a block of ice into each day.

When I was very young we had acquired a homemade ice box that relatives had given us after they bought a new one operated by kerosene. It was a plain wooden chest lined with metal and insulated with sawdust and we kept it in a room we called the "buttery" where my brother had bored a hole in the floor to drain the melting ice. Before we had the icebox, the only way to keep things cool in summer was to store them in the cellar which had an earthen floor, so it was a welcome change to have cool drinks, solid butter, and even homemade ice cream occasionally.

Our ice house was only a short distance from the house, near the front yard. This boxlike structure, about 15 feet square, had a nearly flat roof and a doorway, without a door, facing the North. Inside were piles and piles of the 12" cubes of ice my brothers had cut and stacked there the previous February. They had spread lots of sawdust between the layers which insulated them so they didn't melt. I loved to go into the ice house on hot summer days to cool off, and sometimes on Sunday afternoons I took a magazine to read there and a stool to sit on. Even though I knew that the pond the ice came from was not noted for being clean, and the sawdust was hardly sterile, I could not resist the temptation to chip off a piece of ice with a screwdriver and suck on it or put it in my shirt pocket to keep cool.

By the time I was 9 years old, after a sticky day in the hayfield I dashed to the little stream below our house and plunged into the fast-running cold water with great relief. The year I turned 12, I decided, without telling anyone, to run up the logging roads beyond our house to the pond that supplied our ice. Finding my way through the woods alone was a bit scary the first time, but once I had taken a dip in the cool pond and felt the hot sweat and hay chaff wash away, I knew I would go there often. The water was so refreshing, it was always difficult to cut my cool bath short in order to find my way home before dark.

One evening, just as I started home from the pond, thunder suddenly began to rumble in the distance behind me and the sky quickly darkened. As I trotted along the dusky trail, a bobcat let out a piercing howl only a short distance ahead of me. With my heart pounding, I stopped and calculated which direction would be safest. As the lightning grew brighter behind me, the decision was quickly made-braving the cat would be the better choice. I had never heard of a bobcat attack but had often heard tales of people's adventures with lightning. Fortunately, the cat was bluffing and didn't appear but probably kept a close eye on me as I ran by, breaking all marathon records. By the time I reached home I was out of breath, but felt relieved to have out-raced both the storm and other perils that lurked in the wilderness.

Although the bobcat's screech was frightening, there was little reason to be afraid of animals because very few wild creatures roamed in our neighborhood, and rabies happened only to dogs in the cities. Very few deer, bears, or bobcats chose to live in the woods around us because they had been heavily cut since the time of the first settlers, first to supply the potash market and later to provide grazing space for herds of sheep and cattle. Most of the creatures that clustered around our garden and fields were considered pests rather than dangers, and we were likely to see only porcupines, woodchucks, raccoons, squirrels, skunks, weasels, foxes, and, near the brooks, minks and muskrats, which some farm boys trapped.

None of our barns or sheds were built tight enough to keep out this wildlife, so we often encountered weasels, owls, raccoons and skunks indoors. We all had learned to be cautious whenever we opened the door of our house after dark, too, because there might be a skunk on the porch. One day that summer I helped my brothers take down an outbuilding that was no longer used, and our dog and several cats hurried inside to hunt for mice and rats in the newly exposed areas. When we returned from taking away a load of old boards, we found all the animals sitting in a row in front of the building. We soon found out why. They had stirred up a skunk and none of us could work there for the rest of that day.

On my first hunting expedition in the back field with a gun I had borrowed from my brother, I encountered a skunk. Not wanting to miss, I edged nearer and nearer until I was about a hundred feet away. The creature was the prime suspect in a case involving a half dozen missing baby chicks and the strong odor near the coop was enough evidence to incriminate him. Facing me, he stomped his front feet several times. It should have been a warning, but I was inexperienced. He was quicker on the trigger than I, and the wind blowing from behind him sent the heavy blast of blinding, yellow spray directly into my face. I groped my way home, took off all my clothes, and took a bath. Although my clothes hung on the line outdoors for days, they still held the evidence of the lost battle. It was a long time before my family forgave me, and they never did forget.

Chapter 4

Reigning Cats and Dogs

All of us on the farm were expected to work for our keep, and that included the dogs and cats. The dogs' job was to protect the poultry from invaders, to help drive the cows to and from the pasture, and to signal when a stranger approached. The cats' duties were primarily to control the mouse, rat, and squirrel populations, no small job with all the grain, nuts and other goodies that tempted them to reside on the farm.

We had two dogs that summer, Peggy, a collie, and Duke, a German Shepherd. In addition to their many other occupations, both showed great interest in hunting woodchucks. My brothers were delighted and encouraged their passion because woodchucks were a menace on the farm, digging holes in the fields where horses could easily break a leg and invading the gardens just as we were beginning to harvest them ourselves. Whenever the dogs began their lively woodchuck bark, one of my brothers dropped whatever he was doing and went to help them dig the chuck out of a stone wall where it hid when it couldn't reach its hole. Peggy and Duke enjoyed their role as hunters so much that when the woodchuck supply on our farm dwindled, they decided it was time to help out our neighbor. Apparently Mr. Rogers appreciated their aid, too, because he learned to run and help them out whenever he heard the barking.

One day when one of my brothers was busy plowing a field, Peggy came running up to him, barking furiously. She even tugged at his pants, signaling that something was very wrong. Duke was obviously in distress, so my brother, anxious to help, unhitched the horses, put them in the barn, and followed the excited dog into the woods. When Peggy finally stopped, there was Duke poised immobile, dutifully watching an old abandoned stone wall from which a woodchuck whistled occasionally. My brother, although he was impressed with the dogs' clever teamwork, was not at all sure that their pursuit of a woodchuck far into a neighbor's woods was important enough for him to interrupt his work. We never found out how the dogs communicated to each other that one should stand guard while the other went for help, but never again did anyone in our family question the ability of animals to reason.

Peggy loved every member of the family and became everyone's favorite pet. When my brothers gathered in the kitchen to talk or wait for dinner, they always saved a chair for Peggy who jumped up and sat in it, looking at everyone as if she were part of the conversation. If anyone appeared with a camera, she ran to place herself in front of the crowd and face the camera with a big smile. When we looked through the family album, it was obvious that she was often the only one who looked relaxed and happy.

I always saved part of my lunch sandwich for her when she came to meet me on the way home from school, and I liked to have her trot along when I went after the cows. We could depend on her to bark and alert us when a skunk or raccoon appeared to threaten our chickens or garden, and she even learned to let us know if the stove in the kitchen was getting too hot when someone accidentally left a damper open. Although my brother and his family who lived in the house next door continued to keep dogs, we didn't get another after Peggy died because we knew we could never again find her equal.

There were two kinds of felines on our farm, house cats and barn cats, although the distinction between them blurred, and it wasn't always clear which belonged in the house and which in the barn. The house cats became closer pets, however, and were never as shy as some of the barn dwellers. The two that ate in the house usually went to the barn at night to sleep with the barn cats, and neither type seemed jealous of the other. All of them ate well, feasting on the many mice that lived around the farm, and although we supplemented the diet of the house dwellers with potato, gravy, and meat scraps from the table, the barn cats seemed to thrive with only daily bowls of milk.

We gave the house cats proper names like Susie, Micky, or Tom, but called the barn cats by their color or other characteristics-'Long Hair', 'Scrappy' or similar epithets. None enjoyed the luxuries of kitty litter, canned food, a special bed, or visits to a veterinarian. The barn cats loved the warm cows' milk, and before we got a milking machine, one of my brothers trained several of them to sit upright on their haunches in a line while he squirted milk direct from the cow into their mouths.

Although a few cats were absolutely necessary to the farm, it was difficult to keep the population stable since felines have a way of multiplying rapidly. The females, who were always the best hunters, were each good for two or three litters of 3 to 5 kittens per year. All our neighbors also had an oversupply of cats (one family had 35 barn cats that they knew of) so it was a buyer's market in every way and impossible for us to find homes for any of our surplus.

Not every cat survived, of course. Owls, hawks, foxes, and other creatures sometimes carried off a kitten, and the Toms, who were inclined to wander whenever the spirit moved them, sometimes never returned. During haying the mower occasionally cut into a cat and killed it when we couldn't locate and lock them up first. But worst of all, a few of the fishermen who frequented our brook seemed to feel it was good sport to try out their revolvers on any cat they felt might be competing for the fish.

My brothers had the task of population control for the cat herd. If they found the kittens right away before their eyes opened, they disposed of all but two from each litter which they left to keep the mother happy and healthy, they thought. The more experienced tabbies seemed able to count, however, and often produced their families in one of the many hidden nooks and crannies of the barn. When the kittens were half-grown, they then paraded them out, usually when there was company visiting, instinctively knowing it would be impossible for humans to destroy cute, lively kittens.

In addition to the Malthusian birth rate, the cat census increased in other ways. Romantic Toms sometimes stopped by, liked what they found, and decided to move in with us. Or, occasionally someone would drop off cats in the night near our barn under the misapprehension that farmers needed all the cats they could get and there was always plenty of food to go around on a farm. It usually happened in late summer and we never found out who left them, but suspected that either some village folks had too many cats or that campers at the lake who kept a cat or two during the summer didn't want to take them back to the city. We adopted all newcomers into our large family of felines.

At an early age I discovered that each cat, like each dog, had a unique personality. Some were all business with little desire to fraternize with humans, and they rejected any attempts to make them into pets. Others were eager to spend time in the house and follow me around. I especially liked the tigers, and one little tiger became my special friend. Pierre loved to ride on my shoulder and often came running to ride in the wheelbarrow. He even liked to shake paws with me, but soon gave that up because he was sensitive and everyone laughed at him whenever he did it. He talked a lot and was so good at answering questions that my young niece began to believe everything he said. One day when I came out of the house, she announced from the front porch that she had asked Pierre if I had left yet. He said "no-o-o," so she waited.

The well-known writer Wallace Stegner and his wife had a summer home near our farm and one summer brought two remarkable cats with them. When they left at Labor day, they asked my brother next door if he would like to take the two black and white tabbies, Susie and Simpkins. Since it was one of the rare times when we had only a few cats on the farm, my brother agreed to take them. Simpkins turned out to be calm and even-tempered, but Susie was high-strung and feisty, a type-A character. Within a few weeks she decided to desert her sister and my brother's family and move in with us, completely uninvited.

Although both were clearly city cats accustomed to the intelligence and sophistication of Harvard and Cambridge, they adapted quickly to year-round life in the country. Susie, particularly, loved to hunt and brought us a continual collection of mice, rats, rabbits, squirrels, chipmunks, and even an occasional flying squirrel, a nocturnal creature I had never seen before. She also spent a great deal of time fishing at our brook and hauled back trout, perch, suckers, and other fish that we hadn't even known existed there. Her expertise became very embarrassing for me, because she was a far better hunter and fisher than I and sometimes fetched in specimens nearly as large as she was. The only time she ever met her match was the day she came in smelling heavily of skunk, with one ear torn.

Simpkins, also a good hunter, brought in a lot of loot, but her style was quite different and, it seemed to me, made a lot more sense. While Susie went energetically tearing off at a lively clip, hoping to overtake some unsuspecting creature, her clever sister sat quietly on a rock in the pasture calmly washing her face, admiring the scenery, and waiting for some game to come along, which it usually did. It wasn't long before each tabby had a litter of kittens, and Simpkins then exhibited an even more calculating side. Susie, to feed her family properly, had doubled her hunting and fishing efforts and each day piled up for her kittens three times as much game as they could possibly eat. This bounty did not escape the notice of the opportunistic Simpkins who hid in our hedge and waited until Susie had brought in a plentiful supply of grub. Then, when Susie went off for another haul, Simpkins quietly grabbed a few tasty morsels and took them home to serve to her own brood.

Susie was also clever at figuring out how to make things work to her advantage. She not only learned how to push open the screen door and go out of the house, but she also discovered how the door latches worked. She mastered the knack of turning on the lights she could reach, but she was not a conservationist and we never saw her turn one off. After figuring out that we promptly opened the front door when someone knocked, she decided that if it worked for guests, it should work for her, too. So, with both paws, she would grab the broom we used to sweep off our feet on the porch and bang it hard against the door several times. We always jumped at the noise and let her in promptly.

Since we rarely had company in the evening, we began to expect that when there was a knock at that time, we would find Susie there. One night after dark I opened the door at the knock and yelled, "Get yourself in here this minute and stop making all that racket." Instead of Susie, a rather shocked young hunter who was lost stood on the porch. We gave him a cup of coffee and headed him in the direction of the farm he was looking for, but I suspect he never really believed that I actually thought a cat was knocking on the door.

Susie had a wry sense of humor, particularly when we had guests. She knew it bothered us when she brought in a fat dead squirrel and dropped it in front of them, but she seldom missed such an opportunity. She also liked to curl up on the paper and sleep in the wooden dasher churn we had converted into a wastebasket in the living room. When a visitor was sitting beside it chatting, she enjoyed popping out suddenly, like a Jack-in-the-box, causing gasps, screams, and, once, spilt tea. She also liked to hide behind a bush or building and leap out at unsuspecting people as they were passing by. Both she and her grown-up kittens were hams and when anyone was around they performed on fences, the clothesline, and the bars we used for gates, by running along and pretending to lose their balance. Then they would catch themselves by their front paws and meow loudly while swinging precariously, before pulling themselves back up with a smirk. They practically took bows at the end of their performance.

Cats on the farm faced many hazards, and it sometimes seemed to me that whenever I became attached to one, something happened to it. Susie, however, to my great delight, lived each of her nine lives to the hilt, and we never had another quite like her. Like the horses and dogs, she and her feline friends became much more a part of the family than the unnamed cows, chickens, and pigs. They were much smarter, too, although it seemed, at times, that they were a bit too conniving.

Chapter 5

Yankee Talk and Tradition

"I don't know where folks from down country got the idea that Vermonters don't say much. All the folks I know talk so dern much, I don't hardly have no chance to speak my piece." Reuben Lovett.

Whenever a group of men got together to help out on a major job, like burying a dead horse, it was a good time to hear some fascinating Yankee talk. Although much of it seemed dull and boring. I enjoyed hearing both the oldtimers' stories about their earlier days and their comments about neighbors who weren't present. Wesley Logan, particularly, always kept me spellbound as he peppered his conversation with unique comments. Like most Yankee talk, his was seldom complimentary. "Their kid is homelier than a bushel of mud," he'd say, or "He's so lazy he married a pregnant woman." He described old Mr. Henson as "Older than the devil's grandfather." His opinion of talkative Mrs. Coomer was equally biting: "Her tongue is hung in the middle and wags at both ends." And he said of the barber, "He can talk the ear off a mule."

From others I learned colorful expressions like "He's meaner than a horse-blanket thief on a cold day," "She could sour milk by stirring it," and "He's proud as a rooster with four feet." The women of the neighborhood had some interesting ways of putting things, too. We could always count on Miz Rollins to say in almost any conversation "What in tunket?" or "Well, bless your bonnet." "Land o' Goshen" was a common exclamation when some women were surprised, and since we had a Goshen township in Vermont, I wondered if they said that there, too. "Land of Middlebury" didn't sound quite right.

My own family had a repertoire of colorful expressions that sounded perfectly normal to us. If someone asked me to toss something, they'd say "Ding it to me!" and a maiden aunt threatened from time to time, "You ought to have your ears boxed," but fortunately she never did it. Young people who were getting "too smart for their britches" were told to "Go chase yourself," or "Go fry your feet." There were also plenty of prefaces like "I snum," By crotch," and "I gory," often used to express alarm at the wretched state the world was getting itself into.

Some of the older men had interesting ways of modifying their expletives when they felt it necessary. If the minister or women were present, Henry Rice said things like, "The old son of a biscuit" and "She's a dirty old basket." Those who were most fluent with actual cuss words usually weren't too bright, and used swearing to cover up their lack of communication skills. Jack Revoir, for instance, tried hard to impress his audience, and after a tirade would look around to see who might think he was doing well. I noticed that his cussing always stopped if a woman appeared, unless it was his wife. Then he let go with very rough language, apparently wanting to prove to everyone that he was boss in his own home. I thought it was very funny that grownup men always called each other 'boys', even if they were in their eighties. It might be, "All together boys, lets give her fits!" when it came to raising the framed side of a silo; or in a square dance, the caller instructed the dancers, "Boys, go 'gee', girls, go 'haw', look out sharp for your mother-in-law." We didn't have cowboys in our region, but some people still said "mailboy" and "fireboy" instead of mailman and fireman. Veterans invariably referred to their former comrades as boys. "Rally Round the Flag Boys!", a Civil War tune, was still popular each year at Memorial Day, and we always sang 'Tramp, Tramp, Tramp, the Boys Are Marching'.

Yankee women could hold their own with any group of females in the world when it came to old-fashioned gossip, but the group of Yankee men easily matched them rumor for rumor. Perhaps because most of what went on in our small town wasn't very exciting, many men developed a knack for embellishing even a dull tale, and a story could improve a great deal in only a few hour's time. One day I was picking up potatoes with a group of neighbors when Bill Macomber, a newcomer to our area, dropped by to return a gasoline can. He spoke enthusiastically about his new venture into dairying and mentioned that he would like to build a new barn in a few years. "It may be impossible, but I really want to produce a ton of milk every day sometime in the future," he said in an off-handed way before he left.

His remark was repeated quite disgustedly by the neighbors, all of whom made considerably less milk on their farms. When Jack Rogers, another farmer, stopped by just to make sure we were working properly, he was greeted with "Whadda ya know! Macomber, that cuss what just bought the Tilton place, was here a few minutes ago, and he came right out and made his brags that he would soon be making more 'n a ton of milk every day. Whadda ya think a' that?" Jack agreed that it certainly showed a lack of realism and he was in for some tough awakening in the future.

Another time I was helping when a group of men were repairing the Rogers' barn. Alpha Rice stopped by while the carpenters were pausing for a smoke and, anxious to contribute to the conversation, he mentioned that he had heard it was going to cost two dollars a day to heat the village school with the new heating system. Elderly Mr. Fogg, the carpenter in charge of the barn work and a bachelor, was visibly "het up" by this news and promptly dropped his square, sputtering about how his tax money was being spent just to keep a bunch of dumb kids and worthless teachers comfortable.

About an hour after the visitor had left, the mailman stopped by to look over the construction. "Have you heard what it's going to cost to heat that damn high school this year?" was Fogg's opening remark. The mailman admitted he hadn't. "It's going to cost three dollars a day," Fogg exploded. "I've forgotten who told me that, but it's the God's honest truth." "Well, who's going to pay for that?" asked the mailman. "You be, by crotch, that's who, and all the rest of us," was Fogg's loud, angry retort.

As the day went on, other farmers stopped by to see how the construction was going and each time Fogg greeted them with the news about the fuel bill, occasionally adding to the figure. By the time the last visitor had come and gone the school's daily heating cost had climbed to six dollars. I had to go to school the

61

next day, so I don't know how high the cost of heating the building had grown by morning, but clearly Fogg believed he was being entirely honest with each accounting of the tale.

Many oldtimers were very witty and told fascinating stories of the days "back when", polished by years of telling and re-telling. Some could make even a short visit to St. Johnsbury, 30 miles away, very interesting and hilarious. But the discourses of others were extremely boring as they rambled on, caring little whether anyone was paying attention or not. They frequently changed subjects as they thought of something new and bragged about all the hard work they had done in their youth, the fights they had won, and the sharp deals they had pulled off. No one interrupted their tedious monologues, but occasionally someone standing behind the speaker would point to him and sadly shake his head. It seemed strange to me that anyone would lie so openly about all his accomplishments to a crowd of people when everyone there could remember how things really happened.

Orange Ryder, a typical bore, attended every gathering and work bee without fail. Whenever the operator stopped the machine during a firewood sawing to make an adjustment, we could hear the yarn he was delivering to the man near him. "So I said to him, I ain't a goin' to do it,' and he said to me, 'You ain't, huh?' and I said 'No I hain't.' and he said 'Well, why ain't you?' and I said 'I'm a gonna tell you why,' and he said 'You be, huh?,' and I said 'I shore am,' and he said 'I wish you would,' and I said 'Well I will,' and so I did. I said to him, I said...."

From listening to the radio I knew there were sit-down strikes going on in Detroit, armies on the march in Europe and the Far East, dust storms in the Midwest, and daring aviators making new records all over the globe, but our little world seemed to be absorbed in its own gossip and fanciful deliberations.

I learned early not to interrupt the talk and tirades of older men like Mike Reynolds. "Ja hear about old Pete's grandson?" he would say, not caring that none of us had any idea which Pete he was talking about. "He's been fooling around with what's his name's daughter, and that guy who lives where whosit used to live caught him, right in the act." By now it was sounding interesting, but that didn't matter as it was always impossible to get any accurate details as he rambled on. "You know, he's the same critter that got drunk at Phil's auction some years ago. He's the one." His news was always peppered with a lot of "such a matters" and "and the like o that," but we usually had no idea who he was talking about. Usually it was best to just nod knowingly and let him ramble on, hoping some facts would finally come to light, because his explanations were no help. Everyone knew we would have to wait for a more reliable source to find out what his 'news' was all about. Mike liked to tell off-color stories, too, and these always gave him a lot of trouble. He invariably began with the punch line and laughed vigorously as he tried to reconstruct the rest. Usually it took a lot of figuring for the rest of us to sort out how the yarn was supposed to go.

Our town was blessed with several old curmudgeons, among them Arthur Miles, an elderly Scottish man with no children. If you greeted him with 'Good morning', you wouldn't be too surprised if he said, "Hain't seen nothing good about it yet." Once someone remarked to him that it looked as if it would be a nice day. "Maybe, but I doubt it," was his curt reply. Arthur was very much the Scrooge in our town, as well. At town meeting he always objected to spending any money on schools, roads, or cemeteries, and he did the same as a member of the church committee that managed the funds. He dozed off frequently during meetings but always awoke in time to vote "no" whenever there was a proposal to spend money.

One time Arthur was putting up a new barn, and had hired several carpenters, and was just getting started on the project when Ed Leonard, the head carpenter announced, "Art, you are familiar with the nail agreement, ain't you?"

Arthur quickly indicated that he was not.

"It's the law that every carpenter can take home 20 nails from the job every night," Ed reported.

"Well, I hain't never heard nothing like that, and I don't believe it." sputtered Art.

"It's the law, and we all intend to hold with it," said Ed, firmly.

Art soon figured that five men taking home 20 nails each night for three weeks would have a serious effect on the keg of nails he had bought for the job, and was turning pale. But all the men were nodding in agreement.

Ed let him stew a while, then said calmly, "Well figure. Each of us have 10 fingernails, and 10 toenails, and we intend to take them home every night."

After Art calmed down, he seemed to enjoy the joke, and reported it for years.

I discovered there was very little talk between the old folks that could be accurately called conversation. Instead, each speaker gave a long dissertation while the others waited patiently for him to stop and light his pipe, and then another would begin. It seemed to be generally agreed, "If I stop speaking my piece for more than five seconds, you can begin yorn." Many spoke in monologues because they were rather deaf and, not wanting to be left out, they rambled on and on with the same old tales that the rest had heard so many times they could easily have prompted the teller.

Whenever someone started one of these monologues I tried to walk away, but if I was in a captive audience-a group working together, sitting at a church supper, or waiting for my brother in the barber shop, there was no escape. Some old duffer was always ready to take advantage of a good opportunity to spout forth. I couldn't resist the temptation to imitate some of the more colorful characters when I was home and they weren't around. My family always pointed out that even a dullard deserved respect if he were older, but sometimes I caught them snickering a bit at my mimics.

Although a few World War veterans lived in town, I never heard them discuss that war. But the Civil War veterans apparently had talked frequently about their adventures because their sons were still relating exciting stories that their fathers had told about the war and life in the camps. Our tiny town had sent about 100 men, and more than a third of them never came back. At a young age I had become very familiar with Gettysburg, since both my grandfather and great uncle had been there. The latter had a large family, including several very young children at that time, showing just how determined men were to march off to fight the South. Most of them had never been much more than yelling distance away from home before they left.

Many of the wounded who returned to Vermont had been treated either with laudanum, a mixture of opium and alcohol, or with morphine, and they had become addicted. As use of the drugs became widespread they were made illegal, and a brisk underground business with nearby Canada ensued. Since leather boots were a favorite place to stash the contraband when crossing the border, everyone around us was familiar with the term 'bootlegger'. Apparently some of their descendants had picked up the smuggling habit, because during prohibition bringing in liquor from Quebec became a big business in our area.

My mother told us that when she first came to town as a young girl to work for my father's family, there were still a half dozen Civil War veterans in our neighborhood. Each month, as soon as their pension checks arrived, they sent off for a case of whiskey. When it arrived by railway express, they got together to play 'Marching Through Georgia' and other war songs on their harmonicas and Jew's harps, and talk about their war days.

She also told the story of one old Union vet in the neighborhood who became alarmed when he noticed that his monthly allotment of whiskey no longer lasted until the next shipment arrived, even though he limited his snorts to one small drink each evening. Suspecting his wife, he decided to put a small mark on the bottle after each nip. There didn't appear to be any loss in volume, so he began to feel he might have been wrong until he noticed that as he neared the end of the bottle, the booze didn't have quite the same kick and the color was becoming lighter. Then he knew his wife had spotted the mark and, being resourceful, had added a bit of water each time, after helping herself. Ma never heard how he handled the dilemma, so we never found out whether he then hid the bottle, or ordered extra for her.

Alcohol became legal after Prohibition was repealed in the early thirties, but the legal age for buying and drinking it was 21, so some of the younger men went to nearby Canada to drink, and sometimes smuggled out booze for their friends. People still sang the verse left over from the recently ended prohibition days, to the tune of Four and Twenty Blackbirds...

> "Four and twenty Yankees, feeling mighty dry,
> Slipped across the border, to get a drink of rye.
> When the rye was opened, the Yanks began to sing,
> 'God Bless America, but God Save the King!'"

Since we lived so near Canada, we often heard exciting stories of border smuggling. The shipment of both goods and people were part of the illegal trade with our northern neighbor. Foreigners apparently had little difficulty getting into Canada at Halifax and other ports, and some Asian sailors jumped ship as soon as it touched land, then tried to join relatives in Chinatown in New York or some other city. Though our town was off the beaten track, it sometimes was used as a route for that 20th century underground railway. Dealers in Canada frequently phoned farmers in our neighborhood, trying to sell them hay or wood shavings at low prices, and these pitches made everyone suspicious that they might also be importing live contraband since we'd heard that foreigners hidden in these shipments sometimes got caught.

One day a large open touring car stopped for gas at the station in our village and Mr. Hoffman, the owner, was surprised to see that heavy curtains were drawn over the windows even though the day was very hot. As he was pumping gas into the car's tank, he noticed a small opening in the back window curtain and peered in. He saw what appeared to be about ten Chinese men bound hand and foot with ropes, and stacked on top of each other. As he nearly dropped the hose in surprise, he felt a hard object in his back.

"You didn't see anything, did you?" the driver snarled.

"Not a thing," said Mr. Hoffman, and he never mentioned it to anyone until many years later.

Although our lives revolved around work, I wondered if it was necessary to talk about it so much. Whenever men got together, they always discussed what a body had done and what he had yet to do, and gossip usually concerned some neighbor who either hadn't 'got his work done' or had done it badly. Women talked about their work a great deal, too, since they did very little else. My mother, like the other women in our neighborhood, was always the first member of the family to rise in the morning and the last to go to bed. She awakened everyone else and then began to prepare a big breakfast for the men when they came in from the barn after chores. She packed lunches for her children when they were in school and for the menfolk when they were working away from home. And after the long day of work she always spent her evenings cleaning or mending. No one ever complimented her on her accomplishments, but, like every woman, she was very apologetic if everything wasn't always in apple pie order.

Mrs. Rice used to confide on the party line, "I worked all day in a bushel basket," indicating she hadn't done everything she had planned. Myrtle Smith told my mother one day that she had decided her job for the afternoon was to pile up all she had done in the morning and jump over it, apparently indicating that she hadn't met her quota of work for the morning job. Lily Carter dwelled on the work ahead. One Monday morning on the party telephone line she wound up a conversation with a neighbor: "Good Lord, I just realized, today is Monday, tomorrow is Tuesday, and the next day is Wednesday. The week's half gone, and I hain't got nothing done yet."

A farmer might declare he put in a ten hour day, but he didn't count as work the 3 or 4 hours he spent in the barn doing 'chores'. The long days of hard work in early summer were extremely tiring, especially for the older men, and on occasion some of them would sneak a nap in the haymow or the back forty, always trying to make sure that no one found out about such sinfulness. Once I accidentally came across Mr. Rice sprawled on the ground near a fence he'd been fixing. For a few seconds he couldn't think of an excuse. Then he stammered, "I was scared I was developing a rupture (hernia) and wanted to hold it in place for a spell."

Even though our neighbors worked well together when sawing wood, threshing oats, or helping someone replace a barn that had burned or been crushed by heavy snow, at other times there was considerable rivalry, particularly over their cattle, horses, and cars. Farmers who raised Jersey cows never tried to hide their contempt for Holstein owners, for example. Those with registered animals considered themselves at the top of the heap, while those with mixed herds of Ayrshires, Jerseys, Holsteins, Guernseys, and other breeds were considered near the bottom, at least by the registered Jersey owners. Our herd was all Holstein, but they weren't registered, so we didn't qualify in the competition.

Folks used to tell of two farmers in another town who were always trying to outdo each other in bragging about their superior herds. One Halloween, a large group of boys got together and, after the rivals were sound asleep, part of the group led all the Jerseys a mile away to the Holstein barn, while the other boys quietly led the Holsteins to the barn formerly occupied by the Jersey herd. In the morning the shocked owners were faced with the problem of exchanging their new herds. After sorting out which cattle gave milk and which were dry, they decided the simplest method was to just keep each other's herds. The tale was probably not true, because each farmer was so very attached to his own breed, but no storyteller ever wanted to give up a good yarn for anything as insignificant as the truth.

Whenever folks got together, after they had covered the subjects of work, weather, and cattle, the talk usually turned to how bad things were getting. "Young people are going to the devil," was a common opinion. In spite of their talk, many adults obviously envied their children's new-found freedom and outrageous clothing. A few adult men also began to go bareheaded and wear 'overall pants' instead of the traditional bib overalls. Some didn't wear shirts in the summer, either, much to the disgust of the more proper gentlemen who still wore long-sleeved, dark colored shirts and frayed suit coats throughout the hot summer. A few farmers even purchased bathing suits and ventured into the lake for a swim, but mostly after dark. Abner Hammel was spotted in his hayfield wearing a pair of shorts that he had picked up at a rummage sale, and his cousin Mike wore some colorful striped pajamas that had been passed on to him by a city cousin, having no idea that they were not intended as a garment for the public to view.

A lot of the talk I listened to was about cars. Some folks still drove a horse and buggy occasionally to save the expense of driving their cars, but most had already pulled out the hitching posts in front of their homes. We still kept our post in the front yard, and there were three in front of one of the stores in town to accommodate the people who used their horses for transportation. Even the old horse barn at the village church was falling apart. Old Bill Ryan predicted that those devils on wheels would ruin the country, but most people thought he was simply afraid of driving one.

Some people still relied on walking. The Ralstons, an older couple from a town ten miles away, never owned a car and apparently not a buggy either, because they walked past our farm several times a year when they visited Mrs. Ralston's sister in our neighborhood. We always recognized them coming from a distance because Hiram always hiked about a hundred feet ahead of his wife, Lolly, who followed dutifully behind. As they walked by, often someone in my family told a story about the time Lolly cut her foot badly while chopping wood. Her family didn't think they could patch it up properly so they called the doctor, who took a look and groaned, "That is the dirtiest foot I have ever seen in my entire life." After studying it a bit longer, he added, "I'm willing to bet five dollars there isn't a another foot that filthy anywhere else in the county." Lolly quickly pulled off her other shoe and stocking, and the doctor paid up.

The one time the Scots and Yankees used their cars without feeling guilty was to drive to church. Church was a good place to show everyone that you owned a vehicle. But Sunday was also when we encountered some of the older gentlemen who drove very little, and did it badly. Bruce MacLeod was a particular hazard, especially when he tried to park his Maxwell. Church-goers learned to arrive a bit later than he did each Sunday morning so they could park in a spot far removed from his. They also tried to leave before Bruce got his aging machine in motion, which usually took a bit of time since he had trouble figuring out the gears, and no one, including Bruce, ever knew whether his machine would go forward or backward when he started. About once a month he managed to hit another car, but usually it didn't cause any great damage since he always drove at a very slow speed. I enjoyed making bets with myself over whose car he might bump into as he drove his hazardous journey home.

Driving to visit a sick relative was also acceptable on Sunday, but operating a car for pure pleasure didn't fit the acceptable idea of what one could do without guilt on the Day of Rest. Consequently, when motor vehicles came along, many people felt ashamed about taking a Sunday drive unless they could come up with a good excuse. You could hardly call driving a car 'labor', so the question was whether it might possibly fit instead into the same category as dancing and playing cards, which were certainly not permitted. Gradually, even the Scotch Presbyterians decided that a Sunday drive, after church, of course, was morally respectable.

There still remained, however, the nagging question about whether a pleasure drive met the proper standards for Yankee thrift. Such driving cost money, wore out the car, and had no profit motive. You could consider it some kind of education, but some older folks never got over the feeling that "even ifen it weren't quite sinful, a car ought to be used only for weekly shopping, church, and emergencies."

Bill Morse had no such scruples. He enjoyed driving and since he had sold his farm, he had the time and money to travel a few miles now and then. The year I was twelve, he invited me to go with him to a horse auction in Sheffield. I had no interest in horses but didn't want to miss a ride with Bill, which turned out to be as much fun as I'd imagined. Because he drove around so much, he kept up a running commentary about who lived in every house we passed, and often knew several families who had lived there before the current owners. In only a few hours, I learned who had probably run off with the minister's daughter, who committed suicide by jumping off a high silo, and other juicy tidbits that had happened along every road. A ride with Bill included an education.

Some Yankees, like Bill and his brother Jed, liked to keep up with the times. Jed had heard about people having an "open house" when they moved into a new home. Since the only new houses built in our town were usually summer camps, he decided to invite everyone to an opening for his newly completed sugar house. So in October that year we all traipsed into Jed's sugarwoods and went to our first open house. His wife served cider and doughnuts, and we all dutifully admired the building, which I thought didn't look much different from his old sugarhouse, since it was constructed mostly from the old structure. About the only new thing was the roof, but Jed was obviously very proud of his idea, and it was a good excuse for a party.

Most older men smoked pipes or cigars, but cigarettes were becoming popular with the younger set. Because money was so tight, many of them reserved their cigarettes for the times they were in a crowd that would appreciate their sophistication. Some guys liked to prove they were tough by chewing tobacco and spitting a lot, or by demonstrating how they could roll a cigarette with one hand, cowboy style. Snuff was common with the old-timers, although those who used it often seemed to be somewhat ashamed of their habit. One of our neighbors who indulged always told the clerk in the store where he was buying it that it was for his wife whom he had begged and begged to stop. But everyone knew better.

Woman complained bitterly about cigarettes because the men put their ashes in teacups, house plants, and sometimes the pockets of their shirts and cuffs of their pants. Few local women smoked and those who did seldom lit up in public. Sometimes when we dropped in unexpectedly on my elderly Aunt Rosie, she would be hastily putting away her clay pipe, but we could see and smell the cloud of blue smoke that still lingered in the room. Clay pipes were more popular than corncob pipes, and after they became heavily corroded with soot the smokers put them in the kitchen stove over low coals to burn out the soot and get them back in shape.

I was offered my first smoke when I was twelve. The teenage donor assured me it would take a few cigarettes to get used to them, but amidst the ensuing coughing and choking, I decided that tobacco wasn't for me. I knew I couldn't afford it, anyway, and disliked the idea of stuffing my pockets with the necessary matches and smokes instead of the jackknife, pocket watch, string, and other paraphernalia that I wanted to carry. I was all in favor of smoking, however, since I could benefit from other people's addictions. From time to time the various tobacco companies offered prizes for sending cigarette wrappers back to them. It was no trouble to pick up several empties of almost any brand along the road on a walk to and from school each day. Occasionally, when they were giving a special prize I coveted, like a magic kit, I had to start for school early on a Monday morning to beat other kids who were working on the same project.

Although the men bragged a lot about how they were in charge of their families, most farm women knew how to get their own way. One told her friends that although her husband was the head of the family, she was the neck and could turn him any way she wanted. I used to hear about the time my grandfather built a new bay window on the front of the house. He had no intention of covering it up with curtains or shades, but my grandmother was worried about their lack of privacy with all that glass opening out to the road. After pressuring her husband for several weeks to buy some window shades, she went to visit Lizzie, her sister-in-law, who lived in the house a few hundred feet away.

A few days later when grandpaw was picking up his mail in front of their house, Lizzie came out to chat. "You'll never know how much I enjoy watching you eat supper through your new window, Ephriam," she said. "Every time you bend your elbow, your mouth flies open." That afternoon grandfather made an unscheduled trip to the village, and before dark, grandma had five new shades in place.

There was little crime in our area, but strange things happened occasionally. One teenage boy couldn't resist going into houses when the owners were away, opening drawers and cupboards and rummaging through their things. Since no one ever locked a door, he had no trouble getting in and apparently never stole anything. He was smart enough to never get caught inside a building so he was never arrested, but people saw him leaving a place from time to time which made him the only suspect. No one ever figured out what he was looking for, but the private Yankees were greatly bothered by his actions and some threatened him with bodily harm if he ever entered their home again. He always denied every accusation, but because of his activities the local stores began to supply door locks.

Willie Brice always seemed normal enough in a crowd, but he apparently never wanted to be caught alone out in the open. If he heard a car coming, he would run and hide behind a tree or stone wall, but never too successfully since some part of him was always visible. Some thought he was afraid of being kidnapped, but it seemed unlikely that anyone would want to keep Willie, at least for very long.

Art Walters didn't own a car, and did a lot of walking, too. He was deathly afraid of wild animals, and felt the best way to handle them was to scare them first. On his walks he would stop and yell every few minutes, so we always knew when he was passing through our neighborhood. No one ever became accustomed to his blood-curdling yells late at night, although there didn't seem to be much of anything anyone could do about them. One man said he planned to shoot in his direction the next time they heard him, but it was so obvious that Art's library was a few books short, everyone felt a bit sorry for him.

Growing up with such a variety of neighbors made it difficult for me to distinguish between normal and abnormal behavior. I learned, however, that we had to tolerate the actions of some people, just as we had to put up with chickweed and deer flies. Sometimes I felt others were not as tolerant of my actions as I was expected to be of theirs.

Our news about weddings, anniversaries and other big events came mostly from the telephone party line and the weekly newspaper that was published in the next town. A subscription cost two dollars a year, a price that seemed a bit steep for many Yankees. We heard that when Carrie MacLeod told her husband, Bruce, that she wanted a subscription to the paper, he reminded her that she already knew what everyone was up to. She replied that she only wanted to find out how much stuff people got caught at.

The newspaper editor got his news from the dozen or so "correspondents", who sent in a sheet of all the goings-on that they knew about in their neighborhoods each week. They earned 2 cents per 'item', and some contained real news, such as the fact that the Hilton family all had the measles, or that School District 8 had a new teacher who was boarding with the Rogers family. Other items included the opinions of the correspondents, and we would read such things as "Peter Morgan is painting his house, which certainly needs it," or "The Church Work Committee met with Sally Strong last Monday to plan their year. As near as we can find out all they did that night was play Whist." The most interesting news items were gossipy speculation. "Miss Judith Walker and Mr. Herbert Price spent the weekend in New Hampshire. We expect more details and possibly an announcement following this event in a few weeks."

Court news was usually exciting, too. The county judges were seldom bothered with murders, rapes, holdups, speeders, or drunken drivers, but they were likely to hear cases covering breach of promise, adultery, and alienation of affection. These were always reported with so much delicacy that you had to read between the lines to guess what had actually happened. My friends and I had to refer to the dictionary when the news mentioned such items as bundling, incest, and bestiality, because we could never get the definitions from our families.

The news deadlines came close to the time the paper was printed, and type was set on an elderly monotype machine. These factors left little time for proofreading and the resulting typos made reading the paper much more fun, as long as you weren't the victim of the slip-up. Principal Milton Jones' injury, when he fell from a ladder, was described as a "confound fracture," and in the classified ads Oscar Rice announced that he had a wench for sale that had 'hardly been used'.

Newspaper photos were expensive and once one was made, the halftone was never discarded. A photo of a senior who was valedictorian of his class was likely to be rerun when he bought a new business, and appear again when he won the "Kiwanis Man of the Year" award. The paper might dig it out once again when he retired, and occasionally a photo that was a half-century old appeared over someone's obituary.

The hometown paper always tried not to seriously offend any of its readers since it couldn't afford to have subscriptions or advertising copy canceled. The resulting news was only what the editor felt was fit to print. If a person didn't happen to be around town for a few weeks, the news report might state that he was away for a badly needed rest, even though it was common knowledge that he was somewhere "down country" taking the Keely cure for alcoholism. When a man died, the obituary never mentioned that he had made news earlier in life when he embezzled nine hundred dollars from the county Red Cross during his stint as treasurer and had been through three messy divorces. Instead he would be remembered only as a loving father, an avid fisherman, a devoted Mason, and a faithful singer in the choir.

An item might mention that there was some discussion during the annual meeting of the recently United Church regarding putting a new roof on the church woodshed. Missing completely, however, would be an account of the shouting match between Deacon Dimick, a Congregationalist who wanted to do a job that would last, and Elder Dwight MacIntosh, a Presbyterian who saw nothing wrong with another patch-up job. Reports of town meetings listed only the names of those who got elected to each office and never pointed out that some of the losers got only the two votes he and his wife had cast. The insults that often got traded at the meetings were always missing, as well.

The paper dutifully printed each poem that people sent in, no matter how bad it was. There was a good chance that the contributor, after seeing his or her work in print, would be proud enough to buy several extra copies to give to friends, put in her scrap book, and use for resumes when sending lyrics to magazines. The newspaper never sent the contributor a check for such unsolicited material, however.

Not everyone liked to have his or her name mentioned in the paper, thanks to the persistent Yankee notion that one's name should appear in print only three times-when you were born, got married, and died. One man became so upset at seeing a report of his activities that he threatened to horsewhip the correspondent if it happened again. The writer then made sure that the grouch's name appeared fairly often, and the editor obliged. He knew that even if the grouch canceled his subscription he would probably still buy it for a nickel at the store. Where else could one get such a bargain?

Chapter 6

Rites of Passage

"The old fool don't know putty, and furthermore his horse ain't no brighter than he is. Still his horse knows enough to find his way home from a party." Bill Furney, discussing one of his neighbors.

The party Bill had in mind took place long ago, but we'd heard the story over and over. Ted Waterman had apparently hung around the hard cider jug for too long and passed out. His horse subsequently broke loose from the rail fence where it was tethered and trotted home without a driver. Much later that evening Ted had to be delivered home in a friend's buggy.

Social gatherings, except for work bees, were rare in our neighborhood, and if a farm family had a party it was necessary to have a good excuse. Such events usually happened in fall or winter because in spring and summer everyone was so busy with planting and haying that little energy or time was left for socializing. Still, exceptions were made, even in the busy seasons, for coming-of-age birthdays, wedding receptions, major anniversaries, and the inevitable funerals.

High school graduation was a special event for the few who got that far in school. Even during tough times, families felt that it was all right, for such an important occasion, to spend money on photos, a class ring, invitations, and new clothes. A large crowd of relatives, friends, and most of the rest of the community always attended all three of the graduation events. The first, Baccalaureate, was held in the Protestant church on Sunday night in the second week of June. Eight or so graduates (from the high school population of 35 to 50) proceeded to the front rows dressed in their caps and gowns. The minister gave a sermon geared to them and their future, and the school's glee club sang several songs. The congregation invariably sang the same two hymns 'Lead on O King Eternal' and 'Faith of Our Fathers'.

Class Night, the following Wednesday, was the most fun. It was held on the stage in the town hall which had been decorated with numerous crepe paper streamers. Members of the graduating class presented gifts, gave prophecies, and read a lengthy 'will' to the undergraduates. Each girl wore an evening dress and a single rose that was given them by the school, and the boys, too, wore a rose on their best suits. A dance followed consisting entirely of waltzes and fox trots- no ordinary square dances at this formal event.

On Friday evening, Commencement, the highlight of the week, was also in the town hall. The graduates marched in with great ceremony to the 'War March of the Priests' played on the piano. They sat facing the audience on the stage, along with the school principal, the superintendent, the chairman of the school board, and the featured speaker. Each of the officials parceled out a generous amount of advice to the graduates and underclassmen, and the class valedictorian and salutatarian then gave long talks about some subject that was intended to inform the audience that their 12-year-long education had not been in vain. We could count on the glee club to again offer a song or two, and a talented girl would play a piano solo with a lot of flourish. Finally, either the principal or superintendent passed out the diplomas to each graduate amidst great applause from the audience. A dance traditionally followed this ceremony, too.

Commencement always seemed to be scheduled for the hottest night in June when all the windows had to be wide open, which let in hordes of flies, moths, and June beetles that banged against the lights. When distant thunder and lightning occasionally accompanied the ceremony, everyone was visibly nervous about not being home in case a severe storm struck.

It was not uncommon for at least one woman or girl, and sometimes several, to faint during the long ritual, and occasionally it was a graduate on the stage. I was always puzzled at how easily females could faint, but we got used to one or more keeling over at a funeral or any other serious occasion. We frequently heard that a woman had passed out when she received bad news, such as the death of a relative. Even the comic strips often had a character going PLOP! during any unusual situation. Many women carried a bottle of smelling salts or ammonia in their purses for such emergencies, and my Aunt Sally was never without hers. Although she was a tough old bird in every way, during any visit we could count on her pulling out the salts at least once when she wanted to convey that her delicate constitution was getting more stress than she could bear. Perhaps women considered it proper to faint because they knew they were considered the weaker sex. It was an unusual occurrence for a man, however, and generally regarded as a sign of weakness. During heavy work in hot weather a man would sometimes fall down, but no one ever called it a 'faint'. He just "passed out" for a minute, or he had to "sit down with his whole heft and rest a spell."

Though they were rare, I liked parties better than school functions. Most birthdays were not considered important enough occasions for a party, however. Some farm families celebrated an ordinary birthday with simply a cake and candles at the noon meal with the addition, for anyone under age 12, of a spanking-one swat for each year, and an extra-hard swat "to grow on." No one ever sang "Happy Birthday" or offered either congratulations or sympathy. Gifts and cards were rare, but every year until I was fifteen, my Great Aunt Mary mailed me a dollar which made my birthday a nice event to anticipate. Unfortunately, my family insisted that I should learn thrift early and expected me to put it into the bank rather than use it for all the things I had in mind.

When a boy turned 21 years old, or a girl became 18, it was considered enough of an occasion to hold a party for them, since these milestones were regarded as entrances to adulthood. Neither sex could vote until the magic age of 21, so I couldn't figure out why a girl could became an adult and be ready for independence at 18 but a boy had to wait until he reached 21. It was just another one of those unfathomable regulations of the grownup world.

The summer I turned 13, I was invited to go with my family, one evening in late June, to a party for our neighbor's daughter, Lucinda, on her 18th birthday. Parties were always held in homes unless the occasion was a large one, such as a fiftieth anniversary, which was a rare event. Such celebrations were held in the Grange Hall or our local Community House, a former church used for such affairs.

As soon as we finished chores that night we took baths and changed into our Sunday clothes. I was excited because it was a grownup party, and I knew I'd see my friend Roger whom I'd missed since the end of the school year. I wondered if the Campbells would be there, and if Douglas would bring his accordion. The year before, his parents had bought the instrument for their son who was a bit retarded. It didn't come with any music lessons, but that bothered Dougie not a bit. Armed with his new toy, a music stand, and several song books he toured the town, playing for any and all who would let him in. One day he visited my older brother who was in bed with scarlet fever. We watched him peer at his music rack through his thick glasses, and play with gusto, though the tune resembled nothing anyone had ever heard before. My brother tried hard not to laugh until he had gone on to the next farm, but my mother said the merriment did him far more good than the doctor and all his medicine.

Soon after we drove into the Harris' dooryard I realized that Cindy's mother had planned the customary coming-of-age party, complete with all the time-honored neighborhood rituals I'd heard about since childhood. First, they told us to hurry indoors because it was meant to be a surprise, which I thought might be hard to pull off with a dozen or so cars in the yard. To Cindy's credit, she somehow managed to appear properly shocked and pleased when her uncle, who had taken her to town shopping, brought her into the parlor where we were all gathered and dutifully yelled "Surprise! Surprise!" It was obvious, even to my uneducated eyes, that Cindy was all dressed up, sporting a new hairdo, and had probably known about the event for days. Throughout the evening, nevertheless, numerous people asked her, "Were you <u>really</u> surprised?" and she managed to fib beautifully over and over again, "Oh yes, I had no idea."

Soon Cindy was seated in a large overstuffed chair decorated with pink and white crepe paper, and the evening's program began. We sat on borrowed chairs around the hot, crowded parlor for a full hour, listening to Bob Hawley play his trumpet, 6 year old Johnny Breault recite a cute poem, Annie Morgan and her friend Sue play chopsticks on the upright piano, and Cindy's Aunt Bessie give two humorous readings. Doug and his family did come, but his father fortunately had persuaded him to leave the accordion at home. Cindy's 7 year old nephew, who was learning to play the fiddle, favored us with his version of 'Mary Had a Little Lamb', and 'Twinkle, Twinkle'. His bright red face showed he was probably in as much agony as the rest of us.

Next, Cindy's mother announced that we would all play "guess-that-song." She read a description of a character and we were supposed to fit it to a song title. Unfortunately she had clipped the quiz out of a magazine 25 years earlier and the then-popular songs were so out of date that only a few people remembered them. Most everyone guessed 'Three Little Fishes' when she had 'Two Little Girls in Blue' in mind, and everyone looked puzzled when she said that 'After the Ball' was the correct response to another clue. Roger and I whispered silly answers, such as "Barney Google," to each other, but we didn't dare volunteer any of them.

Following the game we were treated to a rendition of 'Peggy O' Neil' by Evelyn, Cindy's sister, who sang in the church choir, accompanied by Aunt Bessie. I couldn't take my eyes off Bessie's big pug of hair on the top of her head held together with large brown hair pins as it bobbed up and down in time to the music. Following this, Aunt Bessie led group singing which, although only the women attempted to sing, went on and on. Roger and I suffered through 'My Wild Irish Rose', 'Bicycle Built for Two', 'I've Been Working on the Railroad', and 'Sweet Rosie O' Grady'. She gave up only when no one seemed able to handle 'Three Blind Mice' as a round.

Gifts from people outside of the family were not common at these occasions, so we were spared the agony of watching Cindy while she opened and exclaimed over each gift, as my sister said was the custom at kitchen showers for brides. She displayed a few gifts from members of her family that were destined for her "hope chest"-sheets and pillowcases, a pile of dish towels, and a casserole dish. It was customary for each young girl to fill a good-sized box with household items before they said, "I do", and some started collecting their dowry about the time they entered fifth grade.

I was relieved when several women adjourned to the kitchen to prepare food. Roger and I helped the men move all the furniture in the parlor and dining room into the front yard, making space for everyone to dance. A local fiddler, Bob McAllister, provided the music, which was much more fun to listen to than the singing we'd just heard. Bob sat near a door between the dining room and the parlor, and the square dance caller stood in the doorway so dancers in both the parlor and the dining room could hear him. The rooms were small, which cramped the style of some of the more skillful high steppers, but they managed to whirl and twirl around, only occasionally bumping into each other. Roger and I stood around watching them dance for awhile before we moved onto the veranda, waiting hopefully for the food to be served.

After at least two eternities, Cindy's mother and sisters finally announced it was time for refreshments. The music stopped and the best part of the evening finally began. The dancers crowded into the kitchen where card tables and table leaves placed over chair backs, were 'laid out' with plates of sandwiches, cake, and pitchers of lemonade. As usual, I had been warned by my mother to wait until the adults and girls had picked up their food before I got in line, so Roger and I waited as politely as possible, and luckily plenty was left when we finally reached it. We each wolfed down piles of sandwiches made with homemade bread filled with egg salad, green tomato marmalade, and chicken with homemade mayonnaise.

Everyone ate heartily and then sat around and talked until the fiddler played the good-night waltz, 'Home Sweet Home', signaling that it was time for the crowd to depart. Unlike fall and winter kitchen junkets which might last until the rooster crowed, spring and summer festivities ended soon after eleven because everyone had to rise at dawn and work the next day.

In the weeks that followed everyone discussed the party endlessly and concluded that it had been a fine "coming of age" for Cindy. They speculated on how long it would be before she got married, since she had just graduated from high school, but no one was aware of any boyfriends. "A pity, such a nice girl," Mrs. Rice observed. The thought of her becoming an old maid was too awful to contemplate. That wasn't a worry I intended to take on, but I was sure that future coming-of-age parties could be vastly improved if they omitted the long program and just went straight to the food.

We had heard that the Roman Catholic weddings of our French-Canadian neighbors were huge church affairs, and the parties afterwards lasted at least two days. Crowds of relatives from Canada joined the family and celebrated with dancing, drinking, and the singing of old-time French songs. But the weddings of our Yankee neighbors were quite different. They were usually private affairs, attended only by members of the family and the minister, and they took place either at the parsonage or at the home of one of the couple, often in the evening so they would not interrupt a work day. Although we read about the huge weddings of movie stars and high society couples, no one we knew could afford a big spread during the Depression. Sometimes, though, the neighbors would give the new couple a party a few days after the wedding.

June was the traditional month for getting married. Usually the couple tried to keep the date of their upcoming nuptials a secret from everyone and we usually didn't hear about it until after it had taken place. It was common for a group of friends to heckle the newlyweds after the ceremony if they knew when it was happening. They tried to locate the couple's 'get-away' car and decorate it with old shoes, streamers, tin cans and a big sign: "Just Married". Then they attempted to block any road out of town that they thought the couple might take, and everyone chased the pair as they drove away, tooting horns and ringing bells. Few could afford the traditional honeymoon to Niagara Falls, so if they celebrated at all they usually either stayed a few days in a nearby city, drove to Old Orchard Beach in Maine, or took a boat ride on Lake Champlain.

Soon after the couple moved into their new home, they might receive more badgering in an old time ceremony called a chivaree. A group of kinfolks and friends gathered outside the couple's home one night after they had gone to bed. They would then wake up the new bride and groom with horns, drums and other noisemakers, and the tired couple were then expected to get dressed, let in the crowd, and partake of the party foods the crowd had brought with them. The foods at the chivaree were often the only gifts the newlyweds would receive other than items the family and a few close friends might provide, although occasionally a bride might be given a "kitchen shower" to present her with future housekeeping necessities. My mother told me that when she was married in the late 1800s, some neighbors surprised them with a party a few days after the event. At one point in the evening someone suggested taking a collection for the newly married couple, and they passed the hat. Contributions from the unprepared guests netted 37 cents.

It was customary for every new groom not only to pass out cigars to his male friends but also to put an open box of cigars in the local store. This tradition originated, we heard, as a "payment" from the groom to his bride's other suitors for taking the girl away from them. Occasionally non-smokers chose to give away a big box of chocolates instead, and I was always ready to take advantage of that offer, even though I hadn't been a suitor.

I was still too young to attend the larger, more public 50th anniversary celebrations in town, but according to my family they also followed a long standing formula similar to that of Cindy's birthday party. The honored couple was seated on an elaborately decorated "throne" at the front of the hall where everyone could face them. In addition to the inevitable solos, instrumentals, group songs, and humorous readings, there was invariably a "mock wedding". A large man dressed as a bride was paired with a small girl who played the groom. Part of the fun occurred in the "ceremony" when she stood on a chair to kiss her partner. The elaborate cake and ice cream that followed sounded to me like the best part.

Funerals were other important social events, and in a small town where everyone knew each other, each person was expected to attend unless he was in school or getting ready for his own. Even folks who were long-time enemies felt they should go to the service for their adversaries, either out of respect for the deceased, or to ascertain that he was no longer a threat. Because a large turnout was deemed important, the rationale seemed to be, "Ifen I don't go to their family's funerals, they probably won't come to mine."

Church funerals seemed designed to make everything as uncomfortable for the family as possible. The relatives always gathered in a back room of the church while the crowd assembled, then marched in together and sat in the front pews where their grief could be carefully studied by all. Throughout the long service they were forced to look at the heavily rouged body of a member of their family lying in the open casket only a few feet away.

Although I was usually in school during those services, if it was a close relative or neighbor I was expected to go with my family. It was very difficult to sit still through the long service, and I tried to keep occupied by looking at the weird hats on the ladies, and by counting everything in sight. I counted not only the people, but the flowers, the pipes on the organ, the panes of stained glass in the glass windows, and the tin panels in the ceiling. As my skill in mathematics improved, I tried to figure out the square root of the total count, or find how many numbers could be divided into the total with none left over. As a result, my math improved a little but I didn't remember many funeral eulogies. The one for Fred Mulligan stuck in my mind, however.

I knew our neighbor Fred well, and when he died in his eighties he had amassed the largest collection of swear words and obscenities I ever encountered. Furthermore, he was very generous about sharing them. Usually he was dirty and unshaven, and people said he abused his family, causing his wife and even his dog to wear a haunted look. The minister at Fred's funeral was from another town, however, because ours was on vacation. He had never met Fred and only briefly encountered his family. Nevertheless, he was obviously anxious to make a good impression on his first important ceremony in a different parish. After the usual "Let not your hearts be troubled...", the traditional solo, and the prayers, he felt it necessary to eulogize at length and tell us all what a fine man he was burying: "...a dedicated citizen of the community, a loving father, a servant of his Lord, a man who would be greatly missed by all, and what a blessed day it would be when we all joined him in Heaven."

Not only the neighbors, but even his wife and closest relatives looked bewildered as the minister went on and on listing Fred's exemplary qualities. I was surprised that no one walked up to see if that was really Fred in the coffin. His funeral was discussed by the neighbors at great length for many days, and some people expressed their doubts about ever engaging that particular preacher again.

Since most people who died were elderly, it was their contemporaries who were asked to serve as bearers and had to deliver the body to the grave site. It was sad to see the six frail men carrying a heavy casket, and in our local cemetery it was especially difficult because of the terrain. None of the early settlers wanted to waste a good, flat arable meadow for a burial ground, so they had chosen a steep hillside where even a horse-drawn hearse must have had trouble. After one funeral, we saw a man slip on the wet grass and drop his end of the box. Only the quick action of a bystander kept him from falling into the grave, too.

Usually only family and close friends went to the cemetery, especially if the weather was bad, since climbing that hillside was very difficult for the elderly. The nearest storage vault was 30 miles away, so burials took place even in the dead of winter, if a grave could possibly be dug. As I watched the crowd standing in the cold and snow one wintry day, dressed in their lightweight summer suits and dresses, I thought about how terrible it must have been during those early days when everyone went by horse and sleigh.

Friday Murphy was one man in our community who seemed to relish funerals and he never missed one. He had been forced to give up driving many years before because of his indulgence in alcohol, but since he lived near the church he could easily walk to these gatherings. My family, like many others, always arrived at funerals at least a half hour early, but Friday was invariably already there, almost as a professional mourner, sitting in a back seat so he could observe everything. Although he was the town drunk, he usually stayed reasonably sober and quiet for the funerals, but he always cried a lot, even if he hardly knew the deceased. Friday always seemed to be on display in town, sitting on the store steps or on a stump in front of the blacksmith shop, and was often the first person newcomers encountered. In spite of his habits, he lived well into his eighties, spreading sunshine and considerable moonshine, before finally attending his own rites.

Sometimes I heard about an elderly person who was afraid of being buried alive. Stories circulated about this unfortunate happening, and elderly citizens warned their families to get a professional opinion before calling the grave digger. Folks seemed to enjoy telling gruesome stories about people who had dug up a body to move it, and when they opened the coffin, found that the corpse had turned over. With all the worries I had to cope with, I decided not to add that one.

People's attitude about death puzzled me when I was growing up. At the time of death nobody seemed able to discuss it, except in hushed tones. Someone would say things like, "Mrs. Tebbits has passed away, but don't tell her brother yet. We're trying to keep it from him for a while." Why it would be better for him to get the news in a few days, I never knew, or even how they could keep such an event a secret. Families tried to have a suicide hushed up immediately and never mentioned that any death was caused by cancer. That frightening word was seldom spoken aloud though it was a common cause of death for the older citizens. Many regarded it as a "dirty" disease, much like syphilis and similar "social" diseases, and it was especially terrifying because we never heard of anyone who had recovered from it.

Euphemisms for death were the rule. Nobody died. A person "passed on" or "went to his glory," instead. "Jeb Lamson stepped out pretty fast didn't he?" they might say. Horses with broken legs or sick dogs were seldom killed, but were "put down," "put to sleep" or "laid away". Even pigs were "made into meat," rather than killed or butchered. Of all the folks I knew, only the Coomers seemed to be able to handle the idea of death directly, and even they used euphemisms. The boys were very likely to break such news with, "Ja hear old man Carson kicked the bucket yesterday, huh?"

Even if the old Yankees couldn't bring themselves to say the word, death was a source of deep fascination, and after a funeral they seemed to enjoy discussing it at great length. At nearly any gathering, the final days of someone who died long ago were sure to come up for discussion, climaxing in the funeral. People would remember in detail the number of flower sprays, the price of the casket, and the size of the crowd, all of which seemed to indicate the status of the deceased in the community. They also discussed the quality of the soloist's voice, how natural or awful the deceased looked, which relatives didn't show up, and who cried and who did not.

Since most people died at home, their "dying words" were often quoted with great emotion, and many old folks tried very hard to have something highly quotable ready to whisper at the end. Some individuals, on their death beds, made members of their family promise something or other that would, subsequently, be very difficult for them to do. We heard of men who never married, or who stayed on a worn-out farm all their lives because a parent had exacted such a vow in his or her final moments.

In my early days, the funerals I attended were all for elderly relatives or neighbors, so it was a shock when one of my fourteen year old schoolmates drowned while swimming at the lake one Sunday afternoon. The church was packed with young people, and the service was very moving. The girls cried openly, but we boys had been carefully taught not to show our feelings in public. But I was very disgusted with the people outside the church after the service who speculated about the reasons that he, a good swimmer, might have died. Had he been drinking? Did he eat a big meal first? Did he do it deliberately?

Rumors of all sorts spread easily when someone died, and bad ones, especially, circulated rapidly. When a polio epidemic struck our town, crippling both young and old, no one knew where the new disease had come from or how it was transmitted. Invariably the victim's lifestyle became suspect. One man was sure that a local boy became infected when cleaning out the horse stalls and wheeling out the manure behind the cows. A crippled girl was rumored to secretly have had a baby. After a woman who was vacationing at the lake died, nearly everyone gave up swimming there for the rest of that summer.

Our neighbors were fascinated with any unpleasant happening and it was seldom enough to just hear or read about it. If there had been a suicide, accidental farm death or even an automobile accident, for several days people would drive for miles to look at the spot where it happened. If a home or barn burned, people who didn't get to the fire when it was raging would go later to gaze at the standing chimney and cellar hole. It puzzled me, but folks never seemed to get enough, when it came to bad news.

Chapter 7

Folks From "Away"

"I just love summer. With all them campers in town, there's ever so much more to talk about." Molly Jennings.

Lots of people felt the same way as Molly. Much more activity went on when hordes of new and decidedly different individuals descended on our little town during July and August each year, multiplying the population more than tenfold. We called the cottages scattered around the lake beside the village "camps", and the folks who used them, "campers."

A few came from nearby towns, but most traveled from New York City, Princeton, Boston, or New Haven, and some came from as far away as Detroit and California to spend the summer. Many heads of families were either professors from the Ivy League or other universities or prominent clergymen who preached in large churches around the country. Princeton alone had five deans in summer residence at the lake. A man once stopped at a filling station in St. Johnsbury, 30 miles away, to ask how to get to our town. The gas attendant gave him directions, but warned, "You may not want to go there, though. In the summer there ain't much there but a bunch of brainy people."

Many of those brainy people were listed in Who's Who and had won Nobel or Pulitzer prizes. They included advisors to presidents, foreign service officers, well-known writers, and one gentleman who had worked with Einstein. I never felt completely positive about the Mr. Stone who wrote the arithmetic books we used in grade school, even though I never met him. We heard that he occasionally went fishing in the brook near our home, but I didn't care to meet him for fear he'd ask me to do long division or explain ratios. Someone told us that he often used the names of children in neighboring cottages, so when an example said that Henry had 5 apples and Walter had 10, they were real kids. Those of us in the local community should have been more in awe of these prominent summer residents, but most of us didn't know much about what they did when they were back in the halls of ivory, as one handyman put it. The most famous never flaunted their fame and to us they were just campers-different-acting folks from "away."

"Away" was somewhere south or west of Brattleboro, Vermont, which was not the same as "down country." The latter term encompassed geographically the area south of White River Junction, including parts of Massachusetts and Connecticut which Vermonters had been known to visit occasionally. To me, "down country" was a collection of textile mills and machine shops where older boys and girls fleeing the farms had gone to work. Since many of my relatives were there somewhere, I felt that most of the folks who lived there probably weren't too much different from us, and quite unlike the campers from 'away'.

The fact that they were different didn't create as much interest as it might have if the Yankees had been the only ones living here. But we also had to interact with French-Canadian farming neighbors and the Italian granite cutters in the next town who were not at all like us, either. The campers affected our lives more than the other "foreigners" because there were so many of them and they were so nearby, it was impossible to ignore their presence after the big invasion during the first week of July.

As a child I wasn't much affected by the annual immigration because we lived 3 miles from the lake and I didn't go to town often. I was fascinated whenever I saw a bona fide camper, and I heard about their strange ways from school friends who lived nearer the lake and the folks who worked for them. When I became 12 years old though, whenever I had time in the summer I walked to town to swim at the lake, borrow a library book, or spend my small change at the store, which gave me good opportunities to look over the newcomers.

Even if I hadn't known most of the local people, I could have spotted the campers instantly by their strange clothing and behavior. Grown men wore knickers and funny brown and white shoes and walked around town carrying rods in cylinder-shaped, canvas containers that I learned were golf bags. Young women

92

wore shorts and sleeveless tops called sunsuits, which some of our elderly women described as "horrid". Prim and proper Nellie Ingalls announced each spring, "I dread the summer. All those bare limbs everywhere!" And they were. Barefoot children and teenagers ran through the street in bathing suits yelling loudly to each other, completely ignored by their parents and oblivious to the disgusted stares of the older natives.

I not only watched them with great interest but listened in on their conversations whenever possible in the store, and as I walked by them on the street. Their language was different from ours. People greeted each other with "Hi", instead of "mornin'" or "yessir." They used strange expressions such as "okay," and "mau--arvelous" in a variety of urban accents I'd never heard before, even on the radio. From them, we discovered we owned porches, not verandas or piazzas, garages instead of carriage houses, and attics instead of shed chambers. Our brook was a creek or perhaps a "crick," depending on the visitor's origin. "Basement", we had always thought, was the correct term for the manure storage space under the barn, so it came as a great surprise to me to discover that there was also one under our house.

Each year they brought in new expressions which probably had originated with a new Broadway show, movie, or best-seller book. Everyone used them over and over as soon as they arrived in town, and they intrigued us. "Ta-ta" was popular one year for "farewell" and "cheerio," another, and then "bye, bye" or "bye now." "But definitely," they used for several years instead of a simple "yes", and "uh-uh" for "no". "Oh really!" meant "Izzat right!" in our language, and "Technically speaking" prefaced every remark for a time, followed later by "As a matter of fact." "Basically speaking" or sometimes just "Basically" were other meaningless prefaces that lasted for years. They also enjoyed tossing around French phrases such as "Au revoir", "A bientot", and "Merci".

A few local people, hoping to appear sophisticated, also tried using the unfamiliar phrases, but they sounded strange in a Vermont accent and didn't create the effect intended. Few natives could master metropolitan dialects, just as very few campers were able to say "ayer" for yes, and "I gory' properly. We all resented the few who talked down to us or greeted us with "Howdy," a salutation never used by Yankees.

Occasionally different meanings for the same word created confusion amongst the campers and local people. Folks from "away" never ate their dinner at noon, the way the Lord intended, but instead served it at night, about the time the farmers were thinking of bedding down, unless there was hay to get in. Local folks believed the evening meal should properly be called 'supper', and was served at five o'clock sharp. Most farmers would have had trouble holding back their appetites until eight. One camper family invited a neighboring farm family they had gotten to know to dinner, but nobody mentioned the time. When the local folks showed up at noon, which they considered proper, their hosts were completely unprepared. Everyone had a good laugh together, though, after they all got over the embarrassment.

The timing on other invitations often presented a problem. To the summer people, a seven o'clock event, or "sevenish" meant between seven thirty and eight, or perhaps even later. To us, seven meant "be there at least ten minutes early so as to be ready to sit down to eat promptly at seven." No one understood the custom of having crackers and cheese and something to drink before dining which led some native visitors to believe, initially, that the hors d'oeuvres were probably what the campers called a meal. Finally, about eight, when the local folks had eaten their fill, everyone was invited to sit down to the delicious full meal. Brice Collier observed, after such an occasion, that they started to eat about three hours after his digestive juices had started to flow.

During the last week in June the main street in the village appeared quiet and mostly deserted, but the next week it bustled with campers coming and going to the store and post office. Most had arrived by train at the other little village in town, and some described their trips as marathons. One family told us that in the early days they boarded the train from Princeton to the Hudson River, took a ferry to New York, then a horse car to Grand Central Station where, finally they got on the train to

Vermont. The journey lasted two days and even then they were not yet at the lake. Our town's local jitney picked them up at the train station, and the driver later returned to the station in his truck to get their trunks. Each camp had a trunk room where they stashed their half-dozen trunks for the summer. Most early camps were simple, single boarded structures, and looked very much alike because the same contractors built most of them. They were heated with a fireplace or a small kerosene or wood stove, and water came from a spring shared with neighbors or was pumped from far out in the spring-fed lake. Everyone hired the local plumber to drain the pipes in the camp soon after they left at Labor Day so, unlike the rest of us, they didn't need to worry about their water freezing in cold weather.

Once they had settled in, most women and children stayed for the entire summer, but some of the men had shorter vacations and had to return home to teach at a summer school or for other commitments. Many of the men who stayed at the lake throughout the summer spent a great deal of their time thinking and researching and writing learned papers and textbooks, and some even built "think houses" apart from the camps for that purpose. As cars became more reliable and roads improved in the late 30's, some men commuted from the city for long weekends. We were all surprised when we found there were families who actually owned <u>two</u> cars!

The town's three small hotels, which most natives called boarding houses, were filled with families or individuals who stayed for only a short time or didn't want to bother with maintaining a camp. If we drove past these impressive buildings, the long porches were always filled with women sitting in rocking chairs. To the distress and disdain of the Yankee women who observed them, they didn't seem to be knitting, mending, doing fancywork, or even reading. They just sat there rocking back and forth, and as far as one could see, accomplishing nothing.

Two farm families on the outskirts of the village earned extra money by serving dinners every night to the summer people, setting out a huge meat and potatoes repast or chicken pie on a large table, family style. These meals always attracted large crowds, and some families made reservations a year ahead. The farm wives were very busy, because in addition to preparing the meals for guests, they also had to feed and care for their own families during haying season. One of their husbands told us he'd be glad when summer was over so he "didn't have to eat alone in the kitchen no more."

Each summer day the main street in the village was filled with various vehicles that served the campers-meat carts, ice wagons, grocery vans, and a milk delivery truck. They delivered their goods around the lake, because many of the early campers had no car. Those that arrived by train either walked, rode bicycles, or traveled to the village by rowboat or canoe.

One day at church a big black limousine pulled up in front with a chauffeur at the wheel. He was wearing a snappy black uniform, dark glasses, visored cap, and long black leather gloves. In the back seat sat a grand-looking dowager with an elegant hairdo, dressed in black lace and strings of pearls, and holding a set of spectacles on a stick. The chauffeur hopped out, opened the door for the lady, handed her a huge hat, and escorted her to the church door. I stared, but was certainly not the only one gazing at her with interest. It didn't matter because the lady didn't seem to notice. She looked so much like the characters in the comic strip, "Bringing Up Father" that we discussed her for weeks, and began to realize that the world we were reading about wasn't pure fantasy.

One day we watched a man dressed in fancy clothes riding down main street on a saddle horse. He wore a cowboy hat, embroidered boots, and spurs and looked so stern that no one dared to snicker, even though he seemed outlandish to those of us accustomed to seeing only farm boys riding bareback on the backroads. The following Sunday, we were surprised to see him giving the sermon in church, and to learn that he was a famous preacher in New York.

The farmers sputtered a lot about the odd gentlemen who, after they left the store or post office, paused in the middle of the street to read their New York newspapers, completely ignoring the cars that drove around them. Equally condemned in the back country were those who stopped their cars at the intersection to chat with each other, oblivious to the small traffic jam they had created.

We had heard in the comic books about absent-minded professors who couldn't find their way home, and occasionally we encountered the real thing. One day I saw a man carrying his mail from the post office which was located in a corner of one of the stores. He kept getting into one car after another that was parked in front, while his wife kept yelling at him from theirs. In one vehicle he demanded of a surprised local woman, "What are you doing in our car?" She said she was just about to ask him the same question.

The campers had plenty of chance to complain about the year-round residents, too. Each morning, about the time the early risers were going to pick up their mail, a farmer who lived on the edge of the village drove his large herd of Jerseys from the barn the entire length of the main street to a pasture on the other side of the town. Each afternoon he drove them back for milking just as the 5 o'clock rush at the store was in full swing. The cows walked very slowly, backing up cars and dropping little gooey piles of smelly deposits all along the route, which the cars then picked up beneath the chassis, providing a strong aroma to the local color.

I liked to gaze at the clean, freshly polished, brightly colored cars parked in front of the store, intermingled with the elderly black or dark green Fords and Chevrolets of the local folks. The first time I saw a middle-aged woman wearing lipstick get into the driver's seat and drive away while puffing on a cigarette, I was surprised. Though I was no longer sure of what was acceptable and what was not in our community, Molly Jennings, whom everyone called 'Meddlesome Molly', knew exactly how everyone should act. She talked about the painted women and their antics long after summer was over.

One year we were surprised to see an invasion of strange vehicles made partially of wood parked near the store. The campers called them "beach wagons," though I never saw one parked at the beach, which may be the reason the name was gradually changed to "station wagon." They became more popular each year as the roads got better and campers abandoned the slow tedious train and transported their children and baggage from the city by car.

Inside the stores, instead of the men's relaxed winter checker games, there was a continuous flurry of activity as tourists moved back and forth picking up their mail, newspapers, and other supplies. Women, some of them rather plump, sat in shorts at the counter of the soda fountain, and when I was nearby I smelled whiffs of powder and perfume. They ordered ice cream concoctions called frappes, which the teenage boys working there during the summer had learned were just ordinary milkshakes. Some lit up cigarettes, holding them daintily between the index and 3rd finger, just like the ads on the back covers of the magazines. Rumors circulated around town that more than a few of these glamorous ladies were also drinking alcoholic drinks called cocktails. The word "cocktail" evoked a lot of speculation, and no one could figure out what a drink could possibly have to do with a rooster's appendage.

Camper watching became a real passion for some of the local folks. Although in summer the two general stores stayed open until eight o'clock every evening and nine on Saturdays, these folks came into the village in mid-morning or late afternoon when village activity was at its height. Mr. Whitman, who had retired from farming, and his wife Nellie, often parked in front of the store and sat in their car for a half hour or more so they could get a good look at the comings and goings of the campers. This habit distressed the storekeepers because the limited parking area had to serve both establishments, and the Whitmans usually had no intention of buying anything. The observations they and the other spectators made, however, provided interesting tidbits for the party lines. "Could you believe one woman I saw yesterday?" Mrs. Whitman breathlessly exclaimed to her daughter. "Her low-cut dress would have made a baby cry."

A favorite drive for many farmers on Sunday afternoons was the seven mile dirt road that surrounded the lake. Few trees hid the lake so they drove leisurely, taking in the sights of campers walking, sailing, playing tennis, cooking lunch outdoors, and other such activities that were foreign to our way of life.

Sunbathing, especially, got a lot of press, and when an occasional bathing suit was flesh colored, some of the nearsighted drivers nearly had accidents.

Most townspeople accepted the campers, idiosyncracies and all, and had a good relationship with them. A few farmers resented them not only because their presence made a trip to town more difficult, but because so many appeared to be relaxing and enjoying the summer at a time when they had to work very hard. One bitter farmer used to drive his manure wagon slowly through town just as most of the summer crowd were coming in for their mail in the morning; others stopped in the store or post office during the busiest time of day wearing their dirtiest, smelliest barn clothes, just to prove they didn't spend the summer loafing. Like most of us, they didn't understand that not all summer visitors were relaxing the summer months away but were busy writing textbooks, doing research papers, and tutoring their neighbors' children.

Duncan McDonald, an elder in the Presbyterian Church, never felt any need to tone down his criticism of either his lazy neighbors or the folks from away. He was convinced that part of the duties of his high office was to keep his flock on the straight and narrow. "They're just alike, the high ups and the low downs," he said one day. "One bunch lives back in the woods, or in town in tenements, and the other critters live high on the hog in cities, but neither does anything worthwhile as near as I can figure. Now, I ain't talking about the teachers and preachers and folks that earn their money proper, but them as don't do nothing but sit around talking or writing poetry or painting colored blobs on paper. They loaf around here all summer, then hoot off to warm places for the winter and do the same thing. They're just like the bums around here. The poor folks are on relief and don't work proper, but I don't know where those city people get their dough. Both groups lap up the booze, swap their women around, and carry on in general. One thing, I will say, is different, though. The rich folks seem to know enough not to fool around with their relatives and have a dozen idiot kids for someone else to support." No one contradicted him because nobody ever got anywhere in an argument with Duncan, but I thought he didn't understand writers. I had wanted to be a writer from the time I learned to read and wanted to meet some of the well known writers who spent their summers at the lake, whether they had sinful habits or not.

One winter a Harvard professor on Sabbatical and his wife decided to brave the northern snows, and they soon became part of the winter community. Everyone liked them, but unknown to the local folks he was carefully noting everything he heard and saw for a novel he wrote the following year. The setting of the novel was Northern New Hampshire but the descriptions of the native characters and the lives they considered secret were so accurate that nearly everyone in the book was recognizable. Consequently, many of the locals felt resentful and betrayed.

The author didn't return for several years and by then the people he'd portrayed had not only forgiven him, but some had decided that it was an honor to be portrayed in a book by such a famous man. Other summer authors must have taken note; however, since, as far as we knew, none of them ever attempted to describe our town in such a graphic way.

A few local folks tried to ignore the outlanders altogether and pretended that all the summer activity wasn't really happening. To avoid the visitors, they either went to the store only when it opened at seven in the morning, or drove six miles further to shop in the next village. Several families gave up going to church for the summer, returning only in September when they could again sit in their "own" pews. One old farmer, when asked what the town did after Labor Day when all the city folks had left, replied scornfully, "First thing, we fumigate, then we get back to normal."

The lake itself became as transformed as the main street in the summer. Ten months of the year, we thought of our lake as a source of water in case our springs and wells ran dry and an endless supply of ice for cutting and storing in the icehouses during the winter. When the water had warmed enough near the outlet it was a fine place to rinse off with a bar of soap after a hot day's work in the hayfield. It was also a good place for fishing with minnows or worms, either standing on the shore or from a boat homemade with cedar boards. On Sunday afternoons in

June as it got slightly warm, people began swimming and, except for the occasional yelling of a child, the place was very quiet. The only activity was the appearance of an occasional fisherman drifting by in a flat-bottomed wooden rowboat.

In July everything changed, and the water became a busy thoroughfare, since the lake was the center of the campers' activities. Many used rowboats or canoes as their transportation to get to the village, and they filled the water with unfamiliar sailboats and brightly painted canoes. Each summer a few more boats with noisy outboard motors appeared, too.

The children of the campers swam at their own cottages instead of at the public beach with us, but we heard that they wore strange gadgets called water wings and some had belts around their waists with large, colored corks to keep them afloat. One year hushed reports circulated amongst the farm families, that two local carpenters had spotted several young children of one family swimming in the lake stark naked!

That rumor shocked many folks, but folks were more amused than upset when a very religious French Canadian lady, whose English was a bit shaky, broke some stunning news in the store one day. Although she said it was too horrible to talk about, she reported in hushed whispers that a famous visiting actress who was visiting on the north shore was bathing each morning, wearing only the clothes that nature had provided. "And, do you know," she gasped, "those terrible fishermens, they are gathering up there in their boats watching her through their bifocals!"

One of the busiest spots in town, once the campers arrived, was the telephone office in a back room of Will Ingall's home. Mrs. Collier, Mr. Ingalls housekeeper, operated a switchboard that connected the numerous party lines covering the town and also linked us to the outside world, when necessary. Since her office overlooked the village center, she could see everything that was happening there and often told callers that the person they wanted to reach was unavailable because he or she was "just going into the store."

Many academics and other campers saw no reason to own a phone for only two months, and they probably enjoyed getting away from one. Consequently, whenever they needed to contact their colleagues or businesses in the city, they went to the telephone office. Getting through to New York or Washington on the phone was not a speedy operation, since Mrs. Collier had to first call a nearby city, then another a bit further away, and so on, until she finally connected with New York, Boston, or Princeton. At any given time several people might be waiting in the office for their calls to go through. It was a cosy place with chairs and even a bed in the corner where Mrs. Collier slept at night, for hers was a 24-hour a day job. The callers brought newspapers to read and munched on the warm, fresh-baked doughnuts which she provided. Some passed the time visiting with Mr. Ingalls, an elderly citizen and noted story teller who was an authority on town history, having lived through much of it.

The telephone office also received telegrams passed on from the train station in the next village. If the recipient of the telegram didn't have a telephone, Mrs. Collier would summon a man with a car, a boy with a bicycle, or someone passing by, and ask them to deliver the message to the proper cottage around the lake. The village children enjoyed the occasional quarter they received as a tip, but the local adults found it difficult to understand such widespread use of telegrams. To them, a wire always meant the death of a distant relative or other bad news.

Those of us who lived in the back country were not only the observers, but frequently, the observed. Cars with out-of-state license plates drove slowly over the backroads and stopped frequently for a better look at what we were doing. It was sometimes a bit uncomfortable to feel ourselves the object of their interest, like animals in the zoo, especially when, as occasionally happened, the viewer had field glasses, a camera, or had set up an easel.

The artists, usually women, were the most interesting, I thought, and they usually stopped long enough so we could stare back at them. It wasn't unusual, on a balmy summer day, to find a woman with a wide straw hat plunked down on a stool behind an easel in our cow pasture painting the scenery. I imagined what might happen if a bull had been in the pasture at the same time, but fortunately for the artist, my family never permitted that.

Sometimes we would find an artist and her equipment parked in the middle of the road which wasn't usually a problem since there were so few cars passing by. After the morning truck that picked up our milk and the R.F.D. mailman had passed through at noon, we couldn't be sure anyone else would be along that day.

I couldn't imagine why people bothered with all that time-consuming painting business. Why didn't they just take a photograph, have it enlarged, and color it at home? It would certainly have looked more like the real scenery than what they usually produced on their easels. One time I wandered over to watch an artist at work near our gate, and her creation didn't resemble any scenery I could see.

The campers gave us our first look at modern art, something for which we were completely unprepared. They put on an art and hobby show each year to raise money for the church, and one year I went with my older sister. An artist who had studied in Paris showed his collected works, including a painting of a large fried egg, warped out of shape, on a plate equally warped, with something that looked suspiciously like three bright eyes staring from the yolk. I had joined the small group of viewers who were silently studying it, when someone whispered that the bearded gentleman dressed in shorts, sandals, and a black beret, standing nearby was the artist. He appeared pleased that his works were attracting so much attention.

The silence was broken not by a local person but a young summer lad who, after a quick look at the picture and its price, exclaimed in a stunned, high pitched voice, "Three hundred dollars for *that mess*!" We all turned to gaze gratefully at him, since he had vividly expressed our collective thoughts. The artist, however, moved slowly away to await a more sophisticated audience.

Most campers were friendly and seemed to respect our way of life. Only a few treated us as if we were peasants who were here only to supply their needs or amusement. The attitude of this minority, naturally, created hard feelings. A visiting minister was one of the worst offenders, and Molly Jennings, who worked for him occasionally, worried that "he might just get his nose caught in the clouds one day." One Sunday the learned doctor preached in our church in late June and prefaced his message by saying he was glad that so many of the summer people had arrived in town early, because he had prepared an intellectual sermon and wanted to be sure it would be understood. The comments that circulated in the countryside during the next week indicated that everyone had got the message, and he wasn't invited back for several years.

Most campers respected country property, but a few obviously didn't understand how a farm operated, or possibly they thought it was open range, like the West, as they roamed over pastures, opening but not closing gates, and letting out cattle and horses. Occasionally a carload of people drove into an unmown field of hay or grain for a picnic, letting their children tramp down large plots of hay which flattened it so it couldn't be mowed that season. A few even left papers and bottles in their wake. We heard that Carl Benson became so "het up" one July after this had happened several times in his scenic hayfield, that he decided to handle it his own way. He didn't call the constable or confront the trespassers, but found out their names, and one Sunday afternoon he and his family went to their private beach on the lake for a picnic. After they were finished, they purposely left behind a generous amount of trash. News of the incident rapidly spread in both the year-round and summer communities, and the Benson hayfield remained unpolluted from then on.

Since the campers needed goods and services, their presence provided jobs and boosted the depressed local economy in many ways. In addition to keeping the stores busy, they bought wood, ice, eggs and maple syrup from local farmers, and employed carpenters, plumbers, and truckers. They paid boys and young men who were not busy on farms to mow their lawns, weed their gardens, and caddy at the local country club. They also supported the churches, the tiny hospital, library, fire department, and, with their lakeside locations, paid a high proportion of the property taxes. Although most campers had more money than the year-round residents, the teachers and ministers did not appear to be wealthy, and some of our friends who worked for them said they often didn't get the final check for their summer's work until after Christmas.

The income was very tempting but some of the proud Yankees found that working as a servant was humiliating. I never heard a girl or woman say she was a 'maid', or a man claim he was a handyman. Most would say they were "helping out someone for a spell."

The summer visitors at the lake soon caught on how to get a Yankee to do something for them. They learned not to ask, "Could I hire you for a few days to dig a ditch for some water pipe?" They got much better results by chatting with a man for awhile, finally mentioning that they needed a ditch dug badly. Then they would ask, "By chance do you know of anyone who could help us out with such a project?" The Yankees quickly learned that the initial discussion was the best time to bring up money matters. "How much could one expect to earn per hour on such a job, do you reckon?" he would say. After a figure was suggested, there would be a pause while the laborer was apparently figuring out how the job would fit in with his other plans. Then he would "allow" that he could probably work it in, but not until the week after next. This delay was a common practice even if he didn't have another thing to do. Mustn't look too eager. That would give the city person an advantage. After the preliminaries, the camper was likely to pretend to study the proposal carefully, then ask if the native would be much offended if he hired someone else who could do it sooner. Discussion then began in earnest and usually the handyman got the job and the camper, his ditch, but not always as soon as he had hoped.

The attitude of the natives toward their work often confused and sometimes upset the campers. Carpenters, plumbers, electricians, and handymen all liked to keep several jobs going at once so they wouldn't run out of work. This meant that they were not likely to refuse any job, but it also guaranteed that nothing ever got finished in a hurry. A man might remove an old roof, pronounced "ruff', from a cottage on Monday for one family, and if the weather looked good, he'd leave that job to build a porch on Tuesday for another. The campers tried all sorts

105

of methods, from shame to rewards, to get a contractor to stay on his job until it was finished, but with little success. Most concluded, eventually, that the workmen intended to do things their own way, and those who expected their free-lance employees to appear precisely when they wanted them grumbled but put up with it. Those with the least patience eventually decided to vacation in another state. A few with larger properties who could afford it, hired a jack of all trades who stayed with them for the entire summer.

Several local women and teenage girls became exposed to many aspects of the more cosmopolitan outside world by cooking, cleaning, and caring for the children of the campers. Before they went to work, most were completely unfamiliar with electric and oil stoves, to say nothing of the pop-up toasters and waffle irons that were beginning to come in. Even more difficult than coping with appliances, though, was adjusting to their new role as servants. They were expected to serve dinner at 8 o'clock in the evening instead of a 5 P.M. "supper", and some felt that eating in the kitchen alone, instead of with the family in the dining room, was degrading.

Thursday evening was traditionally "maids night out", and many single men spent those evenings cruising around the lake in their automobiles, looking over the numerous girls who were out walking, apparently awaiting some attention. Some potential swains would drive around twice, studying all the possibilities so they could make the best selection before stopping and starting a conversation. One of my single brothers never admitted to this type of cruising, but I think he did it, and when he came home late, he never would talk about where he had been. For many males, the trip appeared to be fruitless. One of our farming neighbors complained that he lost out because he had to finish chores and couldn't start his search until after all the willing girls had been picked up by boys who worked in the shops or other seven to five jobs. "Pickins are mighty poor after eight o'clock," he reported, "the ones still on the road are nothing I want to waste my time and money on." His little brother confided later that he thought the problem was that the girls didn't show much interest in him.

I was too young to get in on any of these adventures, but heard that usually after a time or two around the lake, the unlucky fellows would give up and go to a dance together in another town, hoping for better results there. One hired man we knew always stopped at the village store for a bag of peanuts before starting his trip. Unfortunately, his lures didn't work as far as we knew, because he spent most summers without a date, and finally married a girl from the neighboring farm. Some campers brought foreign maids with them from the city, but we heard that they were very protective of them and tried to keep local suitors at bay. One pleasant young girl we saw often had a heavy German accent, and since Germany's aggression was making the radio news every night, local imaginations ran wild that summer. In her spare time she frequently rode a bicycle around the country roads, stopping now and then to look at the view and write or draw on a pad. Rumors quickly spread that she was a Nazi spy, mapping out likely spots where German paratroopers could best land an invasion as soon as they had overrun Europe.

It seemed odd to me, that it was necessary for her to draw maps, when she could have easily gone into a store in the next town and bought a recently made, detailed geological survey map of the whole area for a dime. But there were no better suspects that year, so she became the target of the gossips, and with each re-telling, the accusations became more vivid. She didn't return the following summer which caused even wilder speculations-she had either been interned, deported, executed, or had gone into hiding, depending on who did the telling. No one, as far as we knew, ever asked for the truth from her employers. That would have spoiled a good story.

My older sister worked for one family for several years when I was young, and they and some of their friends visited our farm occasionally. They, like many others, made a real effort to know the local folks, and because of them I found out more about how the campers lived. Some not only encouraged their sons to work on the farms during the summer, but occasionally a noted professor himself was seen pitching hay onto a wagon when it looked as if the farmer needed help.. A few gave money to the girls who worked for them so they could go to college.

Some of the young camper boys and girls told me that instead of playing full time, as we all suspected, they had to attend one lesson or another all summer. They not only were tutored in languages, mathematics, and other subjects necessary for college, but also had lessons to help them excel in activities they did for fun. They took courses in sailing, golf, tennis, dancing, music, swimming, chess and other activities. I wondered if, in their early years, they'd had tutors for tree climbing, snowman making, and marble shooting. Anyway, it seemed clear that every boy, at least, was expected to be the best in everything he did. I began to suspect that their lives might not be as much fun as I'd thought.

A camper occasionally invited a local friend to the city for a visit. Most refused the offer, leery of traveling to a strange place and risk being made fun of when out of their element. One neighbor of ours couldn't resist the lure of a visit to New York City, though. The tall buildings, traffic, and the mixture of races he saw for the first time overwhelmed him, and he never stopped talking about his adventure for the rest of his life. Once was enough, however, and he never again ventured outside Vermont.

One fall, another farmer attended a baseball game in Boston with the local storekeeper. When the pair headed for the station to take the train home the following day, Ed Stanton was stunned when he saw hundreds of men and women on the street heading for work. "What in tunket are all them women doing out here on a Monday morning?" he wondered disgustedly. "Why ain't they ta-home doin' their washing?"

One day when I was 10, a friend of the family my sister worked for landed a small airplane in the field in front of their camp on a Sunday afternoon. She alerted us, and my brother and I went to the lake to see it. I had never seen a plane closer than a thousand feet overhead, so the prospect was exciting. We'd expected that people in our local community would turn out to get their first close-up look at a plane, but a surprising number of campers were on hand, too.

When we arrived the plane was on the ground, and the pilot was wearing a leather jacket, goggles, helmet, and puttees just like in the pictures I had seen in the Saturday Evening Post. He climbed on the wing to get into his small cockpit, and landed and took off noisily several times, giving rides to campers at five dollars each. The rider sat in an open cockpit in front of the pilot just as the passengers did in one of the old Stanley Steamer automobiles I had seen once at the county fair.

During a brief intermission in the flights, the pilot sent someone to the store for more gasoline so we all had a chance to look over the craft at close range. One of the older summer boys was surprised that this was my first look at a plane on the ground and lifted me up so I could see into the open cockpit. I watched the pilot demonstrate how, with a stick and foot petals, he could steer by moving the rudder and parts of the wings. It all looked so frail-just painted canvas stretched over a small frame-I wondered how it hung together, but for many weeks afterwards I built model planes of paper and wood, and read everything I could find about aviation. Though I was firmly grounded in the hayfield, I thought of little else for the rest of that summer except sailing off like a bird into the white clouds and blue sky.

Each summer we were also introduced to the wider world in our church. Each Sunday, a well-known, prestigious minister occupied the pulpit, and it sometimes appeared that they were trying to outdo each other in theatrics and theological knowledge. Consequently, the sermons were memorable and so entertaining that even as a 12 year old I often walked the three miles to town alone to hear them.

Of course I went to look at the people, too. The summer women sported the most outlandish hats I'd ever seen, and the styles changed each year, quite unlike those of the elderly Yankee women who wore the same topper decade after decade. Some of the visitors wore hats so wide I had difficulty seeing the choir which, in summer, consisted mostly of beautiful young girls, some scarcely older than I.

It was easy to spot the men from "away" in church because, although they dressed up as did the year-round men, often they wore coats and pants of different colors rather than the matched ones the rest of us thought were suits. Some even sported white pants and white shoes. A few of the younger ones didn't wear a coat or tie at all, which created more than a little discussion, especially when the rebels left their shirt tails sticking out over their pants. "What next?" Meddlesome Molly was heard to say. "Will they come in bathing suits and breech cloths?"

The summer music was always extraordinary. A woman who, in the winter, was in the chorus of the Metropolitan Opera sang in our choir each summer, and occasionally an organist from New York played, too. The congregation appeared to try to outdo the choir, singing far more lustfully than our old Presbyterians and Congregationalists. The little building vibrated with song.

It was always interesting to listen to the crowd that gathered outside after the service each Sunday. They paid no attention to me, so I could circulate freely amongst their conversations. Many campers planned their golf and tennis games, sailboat races, and other social events at that time, and I sometimes heard little groups discussing which stocks looked good, and who they thought Roosevelt might appoint to fill a vacancy in the Supreme Court. It made listening to the evening news far more exciting.

Occasionally my sister took me to a concert at the lake on Sunday evening, where they played recorded classical music on a large dock that was part of a large estate that belonged to Herbert Terrill. We sat on the shore and listened to the music float over the quiet lake, which acted like a gigantic sounding board. A large number of people gathered, both on the shore and in boats or canoes on the lake. Since it was their dock and phonograph, the Terrills wanted to choose the music, but we heard that the newly formed Lake Music Committee insisted on picking more classical pieces than the Broadway show tunes Mrs. Terrill preferred. Mr. Terrill insisted, however, that each concert begin with the National Anthem, and there was discussion about whether concert-goers in canoes should stand up for the occasion.

Terrill was a self-made millionaire, and his lifestyle was not always appreciated by the intelligentsia at the lake. Unlike the other wealthy folks at the lake who lived modestly, he seemed determined to enjoy and display his success with numerous guest houses, a dance hall, a large inboard motor boat, a chauffeur, numerous maids, and several automobiles. He liked to be first with anything new, and each spring surprised everyone with something unusual, such as the first electronic organ and the latest car.

Although he didn't have a Rolls Royce or other huge limo such as those that the guests at the local hotels sometimes arrived in, he was the first to own a two-seated, two-door car, known at that time as a coach. On the first Sunday after the Terrills returned to town one summer, their chauffeur waited at the church door to pick them up when they exited. A crowd gathered to look over the car, trying to figure out how anyone could ever get into the back seat. Just as the Terrills emerged from the building, however, a two year old boy toppled from the cement platform in front of the church and began to scream at the top of his lungs. As everyone rushed to help, the chauffeur tipped down the front seat, the couple slid into the back, and they drove off before anyone could see how it happened, and the local people had to wait another week to solve the mystery.

The pair always attended church, usually entering late and sitting near the front. Mr. Terrill shook hands with friends all the way in as he proceeded to their pew in front. His wife, in one of her elaborate dresses, occasionally played a large harp during the service. One summer they brought up part of the choir from Riverside Church in New York, and the professional singers filled the church with memorable music that Sunday morning.

Although I seldom could attend, the campers frequently produced plays, musicales and other shows to benefit the local hospital, library, or church. Both campers and natives attended the magic acts, minstrel shows, and concerts of thrilling selections from movies and Broadway musicals. Most of these events took place at the town hall, a large room on the second floor of the school which served as a theater, school gymnasium, and place for town meetings. The colorful curtain on its high stage showed three men being tossed about in a small boat in what appeared to be the ocean, with the waves washing over the boat on one side. The curtain was raised and lowered at the end of each scene rather than being pulled open from the sides, and it was brightly illuminated by footlights when it was pulled down. I tried, unsuccessfully, to figure out how it could be rolled up so beautifully from the bottom, quite unlike a window shade. It worked without fail, although it made quite a racket in the process. Once an actor located at the front of the stage, where he was to whisper occasional asides to the audience, a common technique in the old plays, had to back up rapidly to avoid being hit on the head by the rapidly descending curtain. The first time I saw the curtain I wondered if they changed the scene painted on it for each show, but after seeing it two or three times, decided it was there for keeps.

I heard that professors sometimes gave lectures in the hall for the benefit of various projects, although I only went to one the year my sister took me with her to attend a political debate one election year. I couldn't believe that the men defending their candidates could have such violent arguments during the performance, and then, when the evening was over, walk off together as if they were the best of friends. A similar exchange between any Yankees I knew would cause the two families involved to give up speaking to each other for at least two generations.

I didn't understand what the pecking order was at the lake, but a few campers took their titles very seriously, addressing each other as "Doctor" or "Professor". Some expected the year-'rounders to use their proper titles when speaking to them, but mostly without success. The most prominent shed their titles when they came to town and their down-to-earth attitude won approval from the local folks since few Vermonters believed a body should be called "doctor" unless he could put on a splint or prescribe a pill.

Most farmers who owned the land surrounding the lake became very well off by our standards after selling parcels of their farms to the campers. None displayed their wealth, but instead, promptly put it in the bank. None of them bought fancy cars, enlarged their homes, or took trips, except for occasionally spending the winter in an inexpensive section of Florida. One elderly Scotsman had only a small portion of his land left after selling off most of a small peninsula on the lake, but he still kept a flock of chickens, a horse and two cows. A bachelor, he never owned a car, and his house gradually fell apart because he couldn't bring himself to spend any of the fortune he had amassed to shore it up. Some of the campers, not realizing his wealth was well into six figures, took him under their wing, gave him food and clothing, and transported him to the doctor and to church.

The very private Yankees were sometimes bewildered by the openness and frankness of the campers who seemed to have little hesitation about asking what seemed to be very personal questions concerning their families health and finances. With no apology whatsoever, some would ask middle-aged women how old they were, and inquire how much one's car cost or if their farm was all paid for. "A little bit longer, and they would have known more about me than I did," Sarah Jackson complained after working one summer for folks from "away".

The friendliness of the newcomers also bothered some of the more reserved natives. The Yankees preferred to keep at least 6 feet from each other at all times, and embracing was only for lovers in private. Even a handshake was rare, and greetings were something to get through quickly. Not so with the Italians, French Canadians, and many of the campers. They, the Yankees complained, seemed to enjoy standing only three inches from your face, and as they talked they waved their arms frantically.

In spite of all their differences, when Labor Day came around each fall, most local folks missed the campers and all the activity they brought to town. Still, it would have been pretty difficult to get a bona fide Yankee farmer over age 30 to admit it.

Chapter 8

Changing Times

"The world is going to hell in a wheelbarrow, and it's a shame and a disgrace." The Older Generation.

During the mid-to-late thirties most of us young people thought the world wasn't changing nearly fast enough, but the older folks fretted about the speed with which it was going to the dogs. Even after several years of the Great Depression, adults were more comfortable with the old ways because they knew what to expect and what was expected of them. Their rules might as well have been engraved in stone.

The regulations for the proper way for young people to behave hadn't changed for decades and went far beyond the notion that we should be seen and not heard. We boys were to wear knickers for dress-up occasions and not show up in suits with long pants until we were out of graded school, and neither boys nor girls should purchase their own clothes without an adult's advice. We were all programmed to begin our adolescence at age 14 and get it completely over with by age 18. Boys who started to smoke before 18 were deemed likely to have their growth stunted and were certainly unreliable characters. Girls who wore makeup before that age also had a shady reputation. And young unmarried couples should never go anywhere together without a chaperone.

Women knew what they had to do each day of the week. Monday was automatically washday, Tuesday was reserved for ironing and baking, Wednesday was the day to mend, Thursday to churn butter, Friday to clean, and Saturday to bake again. Sunday was a day of rest for everyone except the men who did chores and the women who had to rustle up a big noontime Sunday dinner. All other household duties, such as preserving food and house cleaning, had to be fitted in during the week.

Many edicts in my family and the neighborhood were intertwined with superstitions. No proper Yankee ever started anything on a Friday because that would somehow jinx the project. Housecleaning began on the first warm weekday in May unless, of course, that fell on a Friday. Gardening regulations, too, were inflexible. Everyone knew that it was inviting crop failure to plant tomato seeds any time other than when they got home from Town Meeting in early March. Most other seeds went into the garden on Memorial Day, but cucumber seeds had to go into their already prepared hills before sunrise on the second day of June, rain or shine, or we'd risk crop failure. The proper time to set out tomato plants was the second week in June unless there was a full moon that week. That promised a frost. And we all knew that the only good time to plant corn was the week that the bobolinks returned and sang their permission.

Our town was changing. New people were arriving to live year-round which was sometimes alarming to the old Yankees because it upset the status quo. French Canadians were buying farms and some of the campers decided they would rather live in the back country in the summer rather than at the crowded lake. When a farm that had been known as the King Farm for a century suddenly became 'the Stegner Place', there was considerable resistance to the change in name. The farm had been occupied by at least five other families since the original Kings, but by some unwritten Yankee dictum, it was designated to be the 'Orange King Place' forever.

When news from the outside world, with its new inventions, music, and other happenings from abroad burst upon our rigidly structured lives, most older folks tried to ignore it, but I couldn't wait to discuss every new idea with my friends as soon as I read it in a magazine or heard it on the radio. The radio, often pronounced "radd-e-o", was becoming an important part of our lives and quickly replaced the old crank-up phonograph for home entertainment. Some people, when they bought a radio that received short wave stations, invited folks without such a luxury to come for an evening and listen. They might hear Admiral Byrd at Little America in Antarctica, or the static-filled voices of "London Calling in the North American Service." All of us followed the Lindbergh trial closely and my family breathed a sigh of relief when Hauptman was executed in 1936, although many were still not convinced he was guilty. We heard about the huge projects Washington was undertaking in an effort to create jobs and get the economy moving. The Golden Gate Bridge, the Hoover Dam, and the Tennessee Valley Project were impressive but seemed too far away to excite us very much. News from Europe was troublesome, especially to those who still had vivid memories of the Great War of 1918.

Few of us could imagine ever actually traveling to England, but it was thrilling to see photos of the gigantic ocean liners in the new <u>Life Magazine</u> and to hear how quickly they made the trip. I followed the speed and endurance record of each new airplane and was excited about the launching of giant dirigibles like the Akron and the Hindenburg. When we saw the pictures in the newspapers of the Hindenburg explosion in New Jersey in 1937, we were all shaken that anything so tragic could happen.

We read about exciting strides being made in science, but the reports sometimes contradicted what I'd learned in school. Our science teacher had quoted from our textbook that an atom was a particle of matter that couldn't be divided further, but the newspaper that same week described huge cyclotrons already doing just that. Charlie McCarthy, Edgar Bergen's famous dummy, reported there were really only two kinds of atoms. "Up and atom, and lemme atom!" and I had fun repeating that line to my friends. One of my classmates announced hopefully that he'd heard about a man named Einstein who had developed a new theory about relatives. And nobody believed the high school graduation speaker when he told us that the energy in a cup of sea water could drive a ship the size of the Queen Mary across the ocean three times.

Our heroine Amelia Earhart disappeared, and within days we heard a ballad on the radio: "Happy landings to you Amelia Earhart". Songs were composed about many celebrities, such as Lucky Lindy, Herbert Hoover, and Casey Jones, the train engineer who became famous for saving his passengers during a train crash while racing to prove his reputation for being "on time." There was even a popular song about Floyd Collins who died after being trapped in a southern cave.

117

Tunes boomed over our radio about the new inventions, too. "My Merry Oldsmobile" and "Come Fly With Me in My Flying Machine" were popular, as well as ballads about balloons, telephones, and motorcycles. Train songs such as "The Wabash Cannon Ball" entertained us during early mornings while we were getting dressed to go to the barn or eating breakfast. They came in amidst lots of static on our radio from faraway Wheeling, Nashville, and Chicago which sent us WLS, a powerful, clear-channel station.

We quickly learned the popular songs we heard on the radio. "Begin the Beguine," "Red Sails in the Sunset," and "When I Grow Too Old To Dream" were some of my favorites, and even though we could only imagine what the big bands looked like, we enjoyed their sounds. We had to look up the word "swooning" when we heard that girls were swooning over Frank Sinatra. To the best of my knowledge, none of the girls I knew ever swooned. Both boys and girls were thrilled to hear the bands of Glenn Miller and Sammy Kaye. The girls learned to dance to swing, and we all gazed at pictures of young men in zoot suits-long coats and baggy pants and long watch chains-although we never saw one. The grownups had trouble appreciating swing and the Latin American rhythms of Xavier Cougat, but they quickly adopted Guy Lombardo's sweet, soft music as their own.

A new teacher at our high school who had recently graduated from college, invited his college band to play at the dance that followed graduation the year my sister graduated. They played unfamiliar songs such as 'Stardust', and other popular dance tunes, and a few college couples who had come with them demonstrated the latest steps. The parents on hand that night who had never seen low dips, cheek-to-cheek dancing, jitterbugging, and other such maneuvers were in deep shock. The jazz blasting from the trumpets and the loud drummer's wild performance grated on country ears that were more accustomed to long silences. Their faces showed their disgust, but the youngsters loved it and as they were leaving the hall, one excited boy asked his father if he had ever heard anything like that before. "Never," answered the man. "But once I heard a truck

118

loaded with hogs collide with another one full of empty milk cans, and that came mighty close."

Each Saturday at noon while we were eating dinner, a local radio station broadcasted familiar live music by Don Fields and his Pony Boys, a nearby "barn dance" band. We especially enjoyed the songs they played "on request" and one of the local boys took a lot of ribbing when everyone heard a syrupy love song dedicated to him by a girl he was trying to avoid. The Pony Boys played a wide variety of music including cowboy songs, peppy dance tunes, gospel songs, and lots of forlorn ballads telling of swains who had lost their true loves and were going to "lie themselves down and die," usually "neath the weeping willow on the hill."

Not only was our taste in music changing, but the local notion of entertainment in general was being transformed. Folks who had never felt the need to go to the movies before, realized they couldn't face their neighbors without sitting through nearly four hours of *Gone With the Wind*. No one I knew had ever expressed an interest in boxing until Champion Joe Louis came on the scene, just as big league baseball had never seemed very important to most of us before Babe Ruth.

Even though each year we became more informed about popular music, movies, and what was happening around the world, the old-time entertainment was still fun. The Turnbells had an old phonograph with a morning glory horn which played cylinder records that looked like oversized toilet paper cores. I loved to visit them and listen to old songs like "Bye, Bye Blackbird," even though they had played them so much, most were no longer completely audible. They also had recordings of several comic routines from old vaudeville shows, and since Fred knew them all by heart he translated the scratchy sounds simultaneously for us.

At home we had a crank-up phonograph that played flat records, with needles that had to be changed frequently. Ours sat on a stand, but some of my friends' parents had more elegant phonograph players in tall wooden cabinets with dome-shaped lids and storage shelves for records below the phonograph. Our record collection, like most others, consisted of cowboy songs, dance tunes, hymns, minstrel songs, brass bands, and popular songs of earlier days including "Old Folks at Home," "Hallelujah, I'm a Bum," and "Big Rock Candy Mountain."

Even as we listened to the old phonographs, thumbed through old post cards, and looked at the old three-D pictures, we were hearing predictions of far more exciting things to come. Popular Science and other magazines promised us television, an autogyro in every backyard, photo telephones, robots who'd do most of the work, radio controlled trucks, trains on monorails, and much more. Even space travel, it was hinted, was likely to be much closer in the future than Buck Rogers' predicted 25th century. Even sooner would come cures for infantile paralysis, diphtheria, typhoid fever, tuberculosis, pneumonia, and even the common cold. And people who took the newly discovered vitamins would probably live to be well over a hundred.

We listened to a lot of frightening news as well as entertainment. Gabriel Heatter started out his broadcasts most nights with, "Ah yes, there's bad news tonight." He usually told of a riot, revolution, or new information of another deadly weapon the Germans or Japanese might be producing. We were warned to be ready for dive bombers, new poison gases, deadly bacteria and even death rays, all of which the Nazis were testing in the civil war going on in Spain. Wars were breaking out in other places, too. Mussolini was invading Ethiopia, the Japanese had once again attacked China and a U.S. gunboat had been sunk in the Yangtze River.

The geography of Europe that we had learned in school, which had seemed so useless, was becoming more real to us each night as we listened to the news. Berlin, the Rhineland, Brenner Pass, the Sudetenland, and Poland were no longer merely dots on a colored map but real places where the action was taking place. I no longer confused Austria with Australia, and began to be as interested in the events in Europe as the activities of Al Capone, the Dionne quintuplets, Clark Gable, Shirley Temple, and the monkeyshines of college students.

A few of my friends became fascinated by the snappy uniforms of the German youths and the Bund, a group of Nazi sympathizers in this country, and they began to imitate them.

They talked about the New Order and strutted around the school yard, but fortunately none could afford the suits and the arm bands were not readily available. They got no tolerance from their parents who had little sympathy for an enemy they remembered too well from only twenty years earlier.

In the mid-1930s, I listened to news on the radio of a big parade of the Bund in New York City, followed by a rally in Madison Square Garden. Jewish women, furious about the treatment of their friends in Germany, pelted the brown-shirted marchers along Eighth Avenue with cabbages and other vegetables from their windows. I concluded that they had probably picked the produce from the Madison garden, that was probably square, and couldn't imagine why anyone would choose a huge vegetable patch as a place to invite thousands to rally. It seemed like a very thoughtless way to treat what was probably one of the city's main sources of garden sass.

With memories of the Great War so fresh, my family, like most others in the neighborhood, didn't trust whatever Roosevelt might be up to in his talks with European leaders. He had promised that our country wouldn't get involved, but not many believed him. More and more, it seemed likely that the helicopter taxis, televisions, dirigible trips, hundred-mile-an-hour trains and superhighways we were waiting for would be delayed by war.

World politics touched our town directly in the mid-thirties. The Communist party had become quite active in our state and two men dropped by our home one afternoon late in the summer with a petition to get their candidates on the ballot for November. My family, staunch Republicans, were not at all familiar with Marxism, but they were not about to sign anything they didn't understand. The men didn't explain the party line or pressure them, and promptly gave up and left. Others in the neighborhood were less wary, and throughout the state the men collected thousands of signatures from people who had never before heard the word 'Communist'.

When the names were published in the papers and they discovered what they had endorsed, there were a lot of embarrassed citizens. Some got quite a ribbing from their friends. "How soon can we expect to see a red flag flying from your barn ridgepole?" the milkman asked some of the signers.

A few weeks later the state offered to take names off the list if the signers would go to Montpelier and request it. Many did, and as an experiment, a gentleman stood outside the door and asked each person to sign a perfectly harmless petition as they left. Many signed on the dotted line without reading the document or even asking what it was all about, indicating that they had learned nothing from their adventure.

The magazines and our radio continually informed us that it would be impossible for us to live truly full lives unless we used the products that made the sports figures and movie stars rich and famous. We heard frequently that eating Wheaties would make us strong, fast, and first to be chosen for the team. Wildroot hair tonic would not only keep our messy hair in place, but would make the girls fawn all over us. Pepsodent Dental Cream would clean our teeth to a dazzling white and prevent the horrible bad breath that we would otherwise have. Lifebuoy soap would fight our equally offensive B.O. Shaving ads promoted a brushless cream for the "One man in seven who shaves every day," and advertisements for soap products warned us that even with the new-fangled showers, soap was still necessary. Cellophane, a new product, was our introduction to plastic. Irma Hull received a bottle of perfume from her boyfriend for her birthday, and her mother told everyone that she knew it was very expensive because it was wrapped in cellophane.

We noticed other changes in the stores. Our local feed store had always sold flour and grain for the cattle and horses in printed cotton bags that farm women made into pillowcases, skirts, drapes, and sometimes men's shirts. But now everything was packed in burlap bags which we carefully took back to the store for recycling, to get the three cents apiece allowed for each one. Our two little village general stores were beginning to display some of the products that movie stars urged us to buy. Nearly every young male, both summer and local, had a pack of Camels or Lucky Strikes sticking conspicuously out of his shirt pocket, and many women were lighting up Old Golds in public, destroying the manly image the boys were trying to project. The girls were also wearing fingernail polish and curled their hair tightly in something called a 'permanent'.

We learned all about the new cars from advertisements. Perfect Circle ads told us how to remedy the problem of smoke from our cars caused by worn piston rings. Most younger drivers I knew completely ignored that useful information, apparently enjoying all the smoke and noise. Bert Noyes claimed he always drove up to a gas station and said, "Fill up the oil, and check the gas." The quality of automobile tires was improving, but flats were still frequent and blowouts were common. Since most people had little money, they tried to squeeze every mile possible out of their tires. Accidents were caused both by the blowouts and by amateur repairmen who tried to fix up their own damaged transmissions, steering mechanisms, or brakes. In any type of collision, it was likely that a fire would start, promptly followed by an exploding gas tank. When Bert Noyes' car tipped over and blew up, he barely escaped with his life.

The women in our town had begun to drive, thanks to the example set by our new minister's wife and many of the "summer" women. Sally George was one of the first of the farmer's wives to get a driving license, and when she took to the road it alarmed many farmers considerably. Ephraim, her husband, wasn't completely comfortable with the idea, either, though he found it was handy to send her to the store when he needed a part for his planter 'real fast'. Sally enjoyed her new freedom so much, she became a real gadder, according to the neighbors, who worried that her housework was probably suffering. Eph seemed to agree. He told his brother that he really needed two wives-one to stay home and another to "run the roads".

Although the new cars and many interesting gadgets one could install on them were tempting, the coming of electricity brought us even more enticements. Still, many folks were so terrified of getting shocked to death that we often heard of people reporting imaginary shocks from telephone poles, guy wires, and radio antennas.

I enjoyed the progress we were slowly making at home with our newly acquired electricity. We not only gained a radio without batteries and a milk cooler, but also a milking machine and, best of all, bright lights. None of us were sorry to lose the constant worry that kerosene lanterns and lamps caused. We knew well the story of Mrs. O'Leary's famous cow that had kicked over a lantern one windy night and burned up Chicago, and were aware that our barn was just as vulnerable. Each new appliance needed some getting used to. The cows had as much trouble adapting to the milking machine as we did, and even the toaster given us for Christmas seemed a little frightening at first.

Some of our neighbors had more trouble adjusting to the new era than we did. When dial telephones finally came to our town, they were particularly confusing. One day, the week after the switch-over to dial, Mr. Whitcomb stopped in to see if we would call the veterinarian for him.

"Won't your phone work?" we asked.

"Well, yes, I guess so, but I had a little trouble yesterday and I'd rather not use it."

We waited to hear more, so he sheepishly admitted he was afraid of the operator, and finally we figured out he didn't know he had been listening to a recording.

"I dialed what I thought was the right number, and this woman came on and said the number I'd called didn't exist. She hinted that I probably didn't know what I was doing, and to call the operator if I had any more trouble. I don't know what that was all about because I thought she was the operator. Well, I dialed again and she came on again, same speech all over, word for word.

"Well sir, I sat there, trying to figure out my next move, and gol dern it, she came on again, said the same thing over the third time, never changed a thing!

"Well, I tell ya, I waited 'til she was through reciting her little piece, which she must have memorized, and then I told her what fer, calling her every name I could lay my tongue to, in plain old Scotch language.

"So you see, I don't dare to talk with her again, because she will probably remember me, and maybe shut off the gol ram phone."

We made the call, and apparently he figured out how to cope, because he didn't ask for help again.

When Bill Calderwood announced he intended to get rid of his horses and buy a farm tractor, it seemed to some horse lovers as if their world might end at any minute. It was even more startling when farmers who had raised registered Guernsey and Jersey cattle for generations and bragged about the rich cream and butter they produced, now took the advice of their college educated county agent and switched to black and white Holsteins because they produced more milk. "Next thing, we'll hear that Deacon Calderwood is taking up strong drink," was one Jersey farmer's comment. "Might as well mix a little chalk with water and sell it," said another in great disgust.

When the dentist in the next town decided to become more businesslike, he sent out in the mail little reminders to customers he hadn't seen for a while. Since Mrs. Rice hadn't visited the dentist for twenty years, she was somewhat taken back when she got a postcard telling her it was time her teeth got a little attention. "I really don't know what to do," she announced on the telephone. "He didn't say whether I should bring them in or mail them in."

Entering the modern age brought about inconveniences to some folks. After the mailman switched from a buggy to an automobile, it was harder for him to keep up with his reading. Mail was something we eagerly awaited each day, although we usually got only an advertisement from a local store, the weekly paper, or a postcard. We all expected that the mailman would read our mail, and sometimes we saw his car parked beside the road as he scanned the papers and magazines. Occasionally he kept us waiting at our rural mailbox while he finished reading a postcard before he handed it to us. When a magazine arrived a day or two late, we suspected he had a story started and took it home to finish it.

According to most old-timers I knew, everything was much better, if not well-nigh perfect, when they were young. The best of all times, according to them, was the era between the Spanish-American War and the first World War. New horse drawn farm machinery was appearing and many homes were getting running water indoors. There were no wars, no income tax, no strikes, no Wagner Act prohibiting alcohol guzzling, and very little government interference. There was almost no crime, and everyone seemed to have a place to live and enough to eat, although little else. No foods were bad for you, and dentists could pull out all your rotten teeth and put in a new set. No one had discovered the evils of tobacco, air pollution, or vitamin deficiency. Although pneumonia, typhoid fever and infantile paralysis were still threatening, scientists had learned to control smallpox. The Gay Nineties happened only in the wicked cities, mostly New York, and had failed to work their corruption into our little neighborhood. Everyone worked hard, and it sounded as if they invariably lived happily ever after.

I couldn't imagine that a world without electricity, radios, and telephones could be as perfect as they remembered. Now my friends and I had no interest in returning to the horse and buggy days and were looking forward to when we could enjoy the independence of owning a car and all the wonderful new things we were seeing in magazines.

Chapter 9

Haymows and Backseats

"The horseless buggy started it all. Now there ain't no telling where the young folks are or whatever they are up to." Sally Perkins.

Getting married was important to the girls in our neighborhood. For most, it was their only goal in life. Without marriage their fate was spinsterhood which meant that their life would consist of working as a hired girl for someone, or, if they were educated, teaching or nursing. Even those careers, the only ones readily open to women in rural areas, were often perceived as temporary jobs, to be continued only if they didn't get married or their husband died young.

The girls I knew talked a lot about their "hope chests", the large cedar boxes their families gave them when they were in their early teens, usually built by a member of the family or a local carpenter. The teenage girls filled them with towels, potholders, aprons, and other items which they made themselves or were given on special occasions. Those items were intended as the girl's basics for housekeeping, following the marriage that she and her family hoped would be upcoming.

Although marriages were not arranged in the formal sense, many parents worked hard to marry off their children. Bill Cutler had seven daughters, and he was always ready to hire a young man or two to work on the farm so they would be near his girls. Bill Wright, on the other hand, had four sons, and he and his wife invariably invited any new single female school teacher for supper. The rumor went around that she often received her invitation before her suitcase was completely unpacked.

Catching a mate was serious business. The local girls greatly resented it whenever a boy went out of town to find his bride. It was equally upsetting whenever one married a schoolteacher who came from down country or "away". Boys in no hurry to settle down learned to be on their guard around girls of a certain age, and the most wary souls avoided going to dances and other social events where they might be considered fair game.

The entire community was likely to be concerned and would work to remedy the situation if a man over 30 was still unattached, in good health, and had a job, or if a girl over 25 was still single. The priest, as well as the Protestant minister and his wife, seemed to feel that match-making was an important part of their job descriptions. The clergy frequently made suggestions to single folks about a possible partner and sometimes arranged for them to meet. If a girl became fond of a boy, she might tell her minister or priest, and he would visit the lad and bring up her name casually in conversation. Often that would get something started.

School dances, local barn dances, and church and Grange socials were common ways for couples to meet or get together. Official dates were usually made to go to the movies, but many in the back country preferred to arrange secret meetings in the woods, and there were always rumors that barns and sugarhouses were common places for romantic interludes.

Most courtships were not entrusted to the lovers alone. Many people in our region still firmly believed that any unmarried young couple should always have an adult along as a chaperone at any event, though they were shunned more and more as young people acquired cars and found it easy to take trips to other towns, out of sight of their elders. Adults watched the young people carefully, nevertheless, and frowned upon strolls off into the woods at a church picnic or evening corn roast. If a young man and girl showed up in public together, everyone immediately thought they must be engaged, a concept often encouraged by the girl. If they sat together in church at a Sunday service, people began making plans for the nuptials.

Although Victorian correctness was slowly passing in many ways, thanks to our increasing exposure to the outside world, it was part of our heritage and affected our lives. Many folks were embarrassed to admit they had been taking a bath, for instance, when they answered the phone. Apparently it was some sort of disgrace to let anyone know you were ever naked. Most country homes didn't have bathrooms, so washing, whether clothes or body, usually took place in the kitchen near the stove that provided the hot water. Some had long tin bath tubs, but others made do with the laundry wash tub. Since it was difficult to cover up all the windows, some people bathed only at night in the dark. Others had someone stand guard in case a neighbor or the hired man happened by.

Many of our neighbors felt that any word relating to sex was unmentionable, and they used euphemisms, whether they were discussing people or their animals. Pregnancy was seldom mentioned, and, if it was, the pregnant woman was referred to as being "that way," "in an interesting condition," or "she probably won't be out in public for a while." They called a bull "a gentleman cow" or a "critter", and mentioned the mating process only in vague terms.

As naive young adolescents, my friends and I were curious to find out all we could about anything relating to this forbidden subject, even though we knew a lot by living close to the animals on a farm. News reports in the paper were so guarded it was difficult for us to figure out what they meant. They never mentioned "rape" but used the word "assault" or "attack" freely."Bundling" was sometimes mentioned as the reason for an appearance before a judge, but the item usually implied that something much more serious had taken place. We would hear "adultery" mentioned in hushed tones and knew from Sunday School that it was forbidden in Exodus, even though we were uncertain what the word meant.

We went to the dictionary for definitions, but unfortunately the writers of our dictionaries must have been commissioned by Queen Victoria herself, because they were not at all helpful. Most words relating to sex were not defined but referred us to another unknown word which, when we checked, referred us to the one we'd looked up first. It was left to us to speculate on sexual terms, and often our theories were pretty far afield. Now and then a seemingly knowledgeable boy tried to set us straight, but his information wasn't always correct. Listening to the conversation of some of the saltier men in town was more reliable, and I got much of my sex education that way.

Though the actual words were unmentionable, there was plenty of gossip about sex. It was common the hear tales of young people taking advantage of haymows, and there were occasional reports of couples caught in compromising situations by the girls' parents or brothers. We heard numerous stories about hired men and farmers' daughters, and hired girls and farmer's sons. We knew that affairs that took place on Sunday afternoon walks or evening strolls were called "grassings." Roger Lincoln warned me to stay away from anything that looked suspiciously like a couple together in the woods or a hayfield. He'd had a shot fired over his head one afternoon when he had inadvertently come upon a pair. He was in such a hurry to get away, he never found out who they were.

Couples often left the hall during intermission at dances to go to their cars, trusting they wouldn't be bothered. Those without cars sometimes used any unlocked car that wasn't occupied, and we heard after one dance that two teenagers were quite surprised when they discovered that the car they had chosen was owned by the sheriff. The officer was not at all amused, but the rest of us thought it was very funny. Occasionally during such an intermission encounter, one of the lovers would accidentally lean on the horn, which always alerted everyone and resulted in some red faces when they appeared later in the dance hall. One night when a horn tooted, the folks in the car facing them turned on their headlights and later told everyone that one of the pair was a local school teacher. No one could prove it was her though, so as far as we knew, she was never reprimanded.

Covered bridges were said to have been fine "sparking places" during the horse and buggy days, but all of those in our town had been washed away during a flood, and with increased traffic, such a spot would hardly have been a safe tryst. Back roads, gravel pits, and schoolhouse playgrounds had replaced the bridges as favorite spots for late night parking and sparking. Those spots were used not only for romantic interludes by courting couples, but often by married folks who were living with their parents and had little privacy at home.

Once a courtship was underway and promises made, it was difficult for a young man to change his mind. We had all heard stories about fathers who, feeling their daughters had been wronged, threatened direct action with a shotgun. In some cases the girl who had been jilted took the man to court, even if she had little substantial evidence of any misdeed. Women did not have all the legal rights that men enjoyed, but a "breach of promise" suit nearly always won them plenty of sympathy in court. One Yankee lawyer launched his successful political career by winning a case for a poor country girl who successfully sued a prominent, rich man's philandering son.

Because of this, we boys were often warned by older, more experienced men, that we could say anything we wanted to a girl in private, but to be very careful about what we wrote. "Letters make mighty interesting reading in court," they explained. One of the county newspapers was inclined to quote an incriminating letter in great detail whenever such a document showed up in court.

"Shacking up" between unmarried couples got the community's blessing only if both members were over 70 years old, and then only grudgingly. It was assumed, usually, that the woman was the housekeeper or that the man was her handyman. We heard rumors that some couples with several children who'd moved into town recently were not actually married, but since common law marriages were generally accepted, this situation was only discussed, and no action was taken.

If an unmarried girl became pregnant, public sympathy was nearly always with the girl, no matter how shady her past. Generally, the male who had been her boyfriend was presumed guilty unless proven innocent. Most felt that the scoundrel who caused the problem should be made to pay, and once, in a neighboring community, the suspected perpetrator was even tarred and feathered. When a boy protested, as he occasionally did, he took a blood test as self-defense. but such tests were not considered conclusive. Jack Hudson, after such an accusation, was one of several local men who decided that quickly leaving the area was a better solution than fighting it out in court.

Unwed motherhood was, however, considered a family disgrace, and more than one of the girls we knew suddenly made a prolonged visit to an aunt or cousin who lived "down country." There, it was rumored, she placed the child up for adoption before she returned. Everyone could then behave as if nothing unusual had occurred.

In spite of the new opportunities that the horseless carriage made possible, unwed motherhood was not common, and most "accidents" were made acceptable by prompt marriage ceremonies. If marriage was out of the question, the price of $300., a very dear sum, was considered the acceptable fee a father should shell out to the mother's family. The threat of this punishment alone kept many active young men on their best behavior.

Although there was feeling against pre-marital sex, most people realized that it was very important for a young man just starting out on a farm of his own to have a family quickly to help him run his enterprise. Consequently, even many of the pious Presbyterians were willing to overlook such a pregnancy as long as the marriage followed quickly and before the birth. They apparently concluded that it was all right for a man to be certain his bride could have a family, before making a commitment.

Birth control condoms were available, but most young unmarried men were too embarrassed to ask the clerk at the village store to dig them out from the drawer under the counter where they were discreetly hidden. Certain married men, who could buy them without shame, did a brisk business providing them to their unmarried acquaintances at a tidy profit.

Abortion was illegal and frowned upon, but far from rare. Old Mr. Simpson would shake his head and mutter, "It's a shame and a disgrace." Teddy Roosevelt condemned it as racial suicide. We heard that some girls drank doses of a tea made from tansy leaves to bring about a miscarriage, but more often a sympathetic doctor quietly performed an "appendectomy", sometimes without the knowledge of the girl's family.

Fear of disease, as well as pregnancy, made most boys behave. A great deal of information kept floating around that was intended to scare us. During my first year in high school someone from the state health department showed a graphic film demonstrating how we could pick up a germ that would disfigure us for life, destroy our manhood, drive us insane, and eventually kill us. The warnings were made even more scary by a film the movie theater in the next town showed one weekend. I couldn't afford the 20 cents price of the ticket, and had no way to go, anyhow, but my older friends talked about it so much I felt I'd seen it.

In spite of all the warnings, a few boys in high school were clients of a local woman of "ill repute," and bragged about it freely. The rest of us weren't too surprised when, after a few months, they began making weekly visits to the doctor. Since rumors went around that some of the prostitutes in town had both syphilis and body lice, it was assumed that their customers did, too. We never heard of any genuine brothels in our town, but everyone knew about the amateurs in the area who did a brisk business. At the accepted rate of a dollar a customer, even a few high school girls found the profession profitable, but not all the prostitutes were young girls. An older woman in our neighborhood casually mentioned to one of her friends, and the story went around, that if a certain part of her body held out, she would have the farm paid for in another four years. There was no indication that her husband was not supportive of her endeavor.

Although conception was shrouded in secrecy and Victorian correctness, the actual arrival of a child was a big event. The father acted much more proud when his baby was a boy, but unless he had already produced three girls in a row, he seldom seemed upset when the new arrival was a girl. We once heard that a man in the neighborhood had thrown his wife down the cellar stairs when she presented him with their fourth girl, but that story was squashed when she emerged from her traditional two weeks in bed completely unbruised and surprised at all the sympathy awaiting her.

Pete Rich was so excited at the arrival of his first son after six daughters that his conversation with a neighbor right after the event was widely reported:

"We just got a new baby at our house!"

"You did? What is it, a boy or girl?"

"Guess?"

"Another girl?"

"Nope. Guess again."

"A boy?"

"Somebody told you." Pete said disgustedly.

After that exchange, Pete was the subject of a lot of jokes. One man claimed that he had asked Pete who the new boy looked like, and Pete looked surprised before shyly admitting that he hadn't looked at his face yet.

Divorces were rare, but there were a few split-ups among our acquaintances as I was growing up, and the woman usually came out the loser. Since alimony was unusual, when children were involved the couple usually stuck it out until they were grown up and out of the nest. When a pair went their different ways, neither usually married again, although the man might then take a housekeeper or the woman might become one for a widower or bachelor. There were exceptions, however. One prominent, well-to-do gentleman in our town had been married and divorced four times. Nobody seemed to mind, perhaps because of his stature, financial condition, and the fact that he had no children.

It was common for a man to "post" his wife in the weekly newspaper if they were separating, and these notices always made wonderful reading. Sometimes, just to be sure everyone understood the situation, he had the notice printed in both English and French. They usually went something like this:

"I Jacob Cross, hereby post notice that after June 25, 1936, I will no longer be responsible for the debts of my wife, Marion. Signed Jacob Cross."

On one occasion a wife, after reading her husband's "posting", put in one of her own:

"You may have seen the announcement that my husband, Oscar Willey, will no longer be responsible for my bills. That is somewhat strange because he isn't even responsible for his own and hasn't been for years. That's only one of my MANY reasons for leaving the bum."

Some elderly citizens liked to say it was the lifestyles of the new immigrants from the cities that were to blame for any sexual

134

immorality in our town, but, when pressed, they had to admit that scandalous behavior had always taken place. We young people suspected that their righteous condemnation of the new mores might even contain a bit of envy. One older friend of my brother told him, "What bothers me most is that the change came too late for me to get in on it."

In spite of the changing times, our lives were still governed by careful consideration of what the neighbors would think, and I wondered as I looked around at my schoolmates, how many of us would grow up to be just as bitter and critical as the old folks who watched our every move.

Chapter 10

Dog Days

"I think they call 'em Dog Days 'cause I'm so dog tired from haying, chasing lost cows, being et up by black flies, and worrying about barn fires." Caleb Waterhouse. "More n' likely its 'cause the whole dang world is going to the dogs." His brother, Mike Waterhouse.

We were told that the term "Dog Days" came about because Sirius, the Dog Star, rose at dawn at that time of year, but my mother's mother who was born in New York City, had told my mother that dogs there were required to be on leashes or confined during that period because of the threat of rabies. Whatever the reason, we all called the weeks from mid-July to mid-August "Dog Days." No one in our neighborhood seemed to know for certain when they began or ended, but when the weather became really muggy, someone always mentioned that they were well underway.

Those hazy, humid weeks were filled with meteor showers and mysterious sounds that traveled great distances. From our front porch we could hear trains tooting in a nearby village, trucks traveling up and down the main road in the valley, as well as farmers far in the distance yelling at their cows, horses, dogs, and children. Sometimes we heard women screaming at their husbands, and afternoon dynamite blasts at the asbestos quarry on Belvedere Mountain. The nights when it was too hot to sleep were unpleasant, and it was distressing to watch heat lightning flashing in distant clouds, knowing a hard storm was probably headed in our direction and we would soon have to get up.

In spite of the heat, humidity, and storms, I enjoyed Dog Days and felt especially close to the natural world at that time of year. I liked to listen to the sharp yapping of the foxes in the nearby woods, especially the barks of the young, and I was thrilled by the occasional piercing scream of a bobcat or the scary shriek of a rabbit that had been caught by a larger animal.

Sometimes, after I went upstairs to bed, I hooted to a talkative owl that lived in the woods near my bedroom window, and when he felt in the mood, he would fly into the limbs of a nearby butternut tree for a short conversation. Then I went to sleep to the chirping of millions of crickets. The heavens often put on spectacular shows for us during this hot period. The full moon in August was always spectacular because it rose so far south on the horizon, rolling up over the mountains facing our house just as dusk began to fall. During those hot, dry days the moon was often a deep flaming orange-red color which frightened some people who interpreted it as a portent of disaster.

One summer when I was about 9 years old there was a spectacular eclipse of the sun which the newscasters told us to enjoy because there wouldn't be another one visible in our area for another century. None of us knew what to expect, and as the time neared, the bright day grew dusky in mid-afternoon and my brothers who were digging a ditch, kept on working. We had just about decided that it was as dark as it was going to get, when suddenly the day grew dark as midnight, as if someone had switched off the sun. I was scared. All the hens raced toward the henhouse squawking noisily, the turkeys and song birds flew into the trees, and when the sun returned, we saw our herd of cows marching slowly toward the barn.

The total darkness lasted only about two minutes, and when the sky became bright once again, the confused hens ventured slowly from their house, the turkeys returned to the ground, and the swallows who had left the telephone wires flew out of the trees. In spite of their instinctive reactions, the creatures seemed as excited as I was. Everyone talked about the event for several weeks.

Some people in our town became alarmed during the meteor showers in Dog Days. Visiting evangelical preachers warned that the stars would fall as the end of the world approached, and this was one sign that obviously foretold that disaster. I knew from reading that there had always been shooting stars, and enjoyed both them and the shimmering Northern Lights, but one night when a meteor as big and as bright as the sun streaked by, I became alarmed. For many nights I worried that one would hit us

138

and my sister didn't help any when she pointed out they were flying about during the daytime, too, even though we usually couldn't see them.

Everyone expected that the animals, and maybe even the children, would act differently when the moon was full, especially during Dog Days. Some thought that older youths needed especially close observance during that time. Emily Ross, who had graduated from high school, told me her parents didn't allow her to go out on dates when the moon was full, no matter the occasion. They may have heard too many romantic songs about the intoxicating effect of moonlight. Folks liked to point out that the word "lunatic" came from the word lunar, for moon, and my family often warned me, I was never sure how seriously, not to become exposed to too much moonlight at any one time.

Maybe it was because we were expecting unusual happenings during Dog Days, but it seemed as if the cattle were more likely to break the fences and wreck the gardens then. Cats tore through the house and barn at great speed, chasing each other and jumping on the furniture, and dogs sometimes ran round and round in big circles as if they were having fits. The folks who kept bees said they were most likely to swarm during Dog Days, but no one wanted to start another hive then since it was near the end of the honey storage season. An old poem warned:

> A swarm of bees in May is worth a load of hay,
> A swarm of bees in June is worth a silver spoon,
> But a swarm of bees in July just ain't worth a fly.

I didn't know whether there was any truth to the 'moonstruck' stories, but it was nice to have the moon to blame it on whenever I misbehaved and got yelled at.

Throughout Dog Days we were particularly aware of the danger of fire. It was not uncommon to see a terrifying red glow in the sky far in the distance on a hot summer evening as a barn burst into flames, either struck by lightning or from the spontaneous combustion of hay. Before I was born, one of our family's barns had been struck and burned by lightning, and my brothers talked about it often during thunderstorms. One time we helped a neighbor toss his steaming hay outside the barn just before it blazed up, and my brothers checked the hay in our barn often, to be certain it wasn't warming to the danger point.

We worried about chimney fires, too, since the cook stove in the kitchen burned heartily throughout the summer. Although my brothers cleaned the brick chimney thoroughly each spring and fall, creosote accumulated from the constant use and occasionally, if we left the dampers open too long, it would catch fire. A chimney fire was always stressful. In winter it was easier to control them because we could put a short ladder into the snowdrift in front of the house, walk up the snow-covered roof, and toss a bit of snow down the chimney to cool it off. But whenever it caught fire in summer, we had to drag out a heavy wooden roof ladder. We then had two choices, either to drizzle in some water, a risky solution since it might crack the hot bricks, or to shut the stove tightly and let the chimney burn. Letting it burn wasn't usually the best choice, because the sparks were likely to scatter over the dry cedar shingles on the house roof and those of all the nearby buildings. Someone usually decided to sprinkle small doses of water into the chimney to cool it down. Then, after it had cooled, we had to climb up on the roof and brush down the chimney and stovepipe to clean them.

Some farmers had connected their barn to the house with a series of sheds so they could walk from the house into the stable to do chores without going outdoors in bad weather. This was a handy arrangement, but it meant that if either the house or barn caught fire, everything they owned would be lost. For this reason, I was glad my ancestors had built our house and barn some distance apart .

On the farms, we were all expected to take care of chimney fires ourselves, just as in other emergencies, since the local volunteer fire department was equipped to handle only fires that took place in the village. They had two reels of fire hose, each on a two-wheeled cart, that the firemen pushed around the village and attached to a hydrant. Anyone out of reach of a hydrant was usually out of luck. Whenever a fire got really underway, about all anyone could do was to salvage whatever was possible. Even those folks in the heart of the village couldn't count on complete fire protection since the firemen were all volunteers who had other jobs, and it always took some time for them to arrive. Some were rather elderly, and fires were so infrequent that they tended to forget the hydrant wrench or some other vital equipment when they ran to a blaze.

After every fire, Deacon Rice, who always had a proverb for every occasion, could be counted on to state profoundly "Fire is a good servant, but a poor master." He snapped his eyes and looked firmly at each of his listeners individually as he pontificated. Everyone was expected to nod in agreement, as if they had never heard his proverb before.

By early August the wild raspberries were ripe. We couldn't always find them on our own land, since they grew best where lumber or pulp had been harvested about four or five years previously. Raspberry plants were nature's way of covering the ground after trees were cut to provide shade for the newly sprouting tree seedlings. The plants produced good yields for three to five years, then died when the young trees they had protected began to crowd them out.

I went raspberrying with my brothers on cloudy and rainy days when we couldn't hay, and since everyone kept track of where the berries were growing that year, we often found others picking there, too. People were always generous about telling their neighbors where new raspberry plants were producing because they were so abundant, and usually we didn't have to go far to find gallons of the sweet red berries.

Berrying was a job I loved, in spite of having to fight my way through prickly brambles, tripping over fallen logs, falling into big holes, and sometimes spilling a pail of berries in the process. When I was younger my family always gave me a stick of gum before reaching the patch, on the theory that if my mouth was full and busy, I'd be less tempted to follow the old rule of "one for the mouth and one for the pail." We always used empty lard pails as containers and they worked well. We punched holes in the top and inserted wire bails to make a handle, and once we were in the berry patch we hung the pails on our belts, which left both hands free to pick berries. Before we started picking, we covered the base of the pail with raspberry leaves to cushion the fall of the first fragile berries. When the pail was nearly full we dumped them into a larger kettle that we usually had placed on a stump. It was not easy to find the kettle among the high bushes, so we usually tied a shirt or handkerchief to the branch of a tall bush nearby as a signpost.

Since it took a long time to fill each pail, we called to each other from time to time to keep in touch and to learn how everyone was doing. If one of us found an especially good place, we'd alert the others. We occasionally heard other people talking in the thick bushes but couldn't see them, and one day we were startled to hear an older man's squeaky voice say to his companion, "How ya coming Phoebe? Have you got yer bottom covered yet?" It was a logical question because the pail seemed to become full faster once the bottom was out of sight, but it was difficult to suppress our snickers.

Bramble patches were not good places to wear shorts, and, as the day warmed, the high boots we had put on earlier as protection against the wet, thorny bushes became hot and uncomfortable. By the end of the day my arms were red with scratches and bumps from the prickly bushes, the heat, and the deer flies. I tried to concentrate on finding berries and listening to the white throated sparrows that always seemed to surround raspberry patches.

I never saw a black bear in the raspberry patch, but we sometimes saw flattened spots where they had torn down the bushes or laid down for a nap between lunches. Now and then on a harvesting expedition someone encountered a bear, and those stories made the rounds. One year while Mary Noyes was busy picking she heard coughing that sounded as if someone were in great pain. Anxious to help, she stood on a stump to see who was in trouble. From her high vantage point she spotted a large black bear busily picking berries only a few feet away from her and occasionally choking on the leaves he was heaving in along with the fruit. Mary said she made a rather hurried decision to stake out another area.

Because the soft, juicy berries were extremely perishable, my mother usually stayed up most of the night picking over our day's harvest. She converted some into jam and canned others to use for sauce and pies on Sunday nights during the winter. We all looked forward most to those she sugared for fresh raspberry shortcake the following day. It was a special treat and made all the itchy bites and bloody scratches on my skin seem worthwhile.

Ice cream was another feast during Dog Days. When I was old enough, I stopped at the soda fountain at the general store and used my precious 5 cents to buy a cone of maple walnut ice cream, one of my favorite flavors, and pure bliss on a hot summer afternoon. It was always tempting to bite off the bottom of the cone and suck out the ice cream, but whenever I tried it my mother didn't appreciate my messy shirt. We made ice cream at home occasionally on Sunday afternoons because we had time then to get the ice out of the ice house, and pound it into small pieces. We dumped it into the old wooden freezer, and then sprinkled salt over the crushed ice to make it melt enough to freeze the creamy mixture which my mother had prepared. It was never difficult to talk me into turning the crank, because I knew I'd be rewarded with the opportunity to lick the float. Turning the crank seemed to take forever, and it required muscles I didn't know I had until they started to ache, but the results were worth the pain. We always made vanilla, but sometimes we added a few wild strawberries or maple syrup. Roger Lincoln's family usually made chocolate and invited me to join them once, but I didn't like the taste or its dark, dirty appearance, compared to our creamy white vanilla.

We didn't make ice cream as often as I'd have liked because, although our Holstein cows produced a lot of milk, there wasn't much cream on it and when we separated the milk from the cream, we needed to churn most of the cream to use for butter. We "separated" once a week and it was also my job to crank the separator. The milk went through a series of cups which rotated at high speed, and centrifugal force pushed the milk and cream out two different spouts, which we caught in different pails. We gave the skim milk to the pigs and calves, and churned the cream. I liked to crank the separator quickly to get the job done fast, but the directions on the machine said "60 revolutions a minute," and any faster speed resulted in less cream. I could depend on my brothers to yell whenever I was churning too fast and the cream supply was beginning to shrink.

My family had given up using the old barrel churn they had used when they were shipping out butter a hundred years earlier, and the old dasher churn had also been retired. We now used a "modern" metal crank churn, and it was my job to turn that crank, too, another long, monotonous job. When I got tired of cranking in one direction I wanted to turn it the other way, but there was a superstition that if the butter was already nearly made, reversing the process would turn it all back to cream. I had trouble believing that, so one day, just before the butter began to form, I started cranking backwards. Just as I'd expected, the butter came out on schedule.

Before haying was done we had to take a day off occasionally to fill the woodshed with all the firewood we had cut and sawed the previous winter, another sweaty job during Dog Days. Since I always looked for ways to make a job easier (I called it being efficient, though my brothers thought "lazy" was a better term.) I never thought it was necessary to pile wood so it looked like a calendar picture, since we would be burning it in only a few months. My brothers, however, felt that anything worth doing at all should be done in the traditional manner, which meant that every stick should be positioned perfectly. They also pointed out that one never knew when an uncle or neighbor might look into the shed, and it would completely shatter our reputation if the pile didn't meet their specifications. It didn't seem to me that our neighbors' opinions were that important, but one day my casually piled wood fell over in a tangled mess. Then, when I found out how much harder it was to pile it the second time, I grudgingly decided that my brothers might be at least partly right, even though their motivations were wrong.

During Dog Days a traveling Gypsy caravan often came to town. They no longer drove their traditional horses and colored wagons, but arrived instead with brightly decorated trucks and trailers. Each year they camped in the valley beside the main road and a small brook, which became both their water supply and disposal site. Their visit often coincided with one of the nearby county fairs where they would sneak over the fence in the early morning and set up fortune-telling booths.

Word of their arrival spread rapidly and even the folks in the back country were on guard because of their unsavory reputation. The olive-skinned men and children circulated around town, selling novelties, and offering to do odd jobs. They tried to get into homes and barns by pretending to buy rags and old junk. It is likely that all the things that were reported stolen didn't actually disappear during their stay, but no one was sure. The storekeepers carefully kept their businesses open for only a few hours early each day when the Gypsies were in town, and then carefully locked up early. The Gypsy children were extremely friendly, but since they, too, had a reputation for being pickpockets and grabbing things, no one would let them near their buildings. Even the smallest of them looked tough, and it was obvious that they had been educated in the camps and had learned their lessons well.

We heard that Gypsies liked to kidnap local children to get "outside blood" into their tribes, but I never heard that any kids were missing after they moved on. Actually, I kept hoping that when they were shopping for new stock, they might pick up a couple of the bullies in my school, but it never happened. Usually the encampment stayed around for only a week before the local constable and county sheriff urged them on.

Though we didn't have many visitors, two who came often were the Raleigh man, who brought an assortment of flavorings and health products, and the Fuller brush salesman, who got into the house by giving away a free brush, one that "every housewife needs". Other men stopped by, including antique dealers, but since my mother had heard many wild stories about traveling men, if she didn't know the visitor, she usually kept him on the porch and made him talk through the screen door which she carefully kept hooked. We had heard that the buying schemes of antique dealers included admiring an ugly piece of furniture they didn't really want while eyeing a more valuable piece. "I could never afford that," they would say about the junk, "but I'll be glad to take that other old worthless piece off your hands," indicating the prize they really wanted. Often this scheme worked.

Sometimes summer campers tried to find ways to get into the farmers' attics, too, claiming they were furnishing an old camp and needed some cheap old cast-offs. We frequently heard a farmer bragging about getting a few dollars for a nice old dresser or rolltop desk, never realizing how much it was actually worth.

One hot, humid August the minister of our church decided to take his mission to the back country, and he got permission to teach Sunday afternoon classes in our little one-room schoolhouse. He recruited about a dozen children and their parents, and I got talked into going although I had misgivings about going back to school in summer. After Sunday dinner I reluctantly walked the mile to school and even more reluctantly entered the smelly building which hadn't been opened for two months and was full of fiercely biting deer flies. The minister was an excellent teacher, however, and many of the children probably never forgot him, as they experienced the only religious training they'd ever had. At the end of August, he presented several of us with new Bibles for memorizing about 20 passages.

It was difficult not to envy the kids who could spend every Sunday afternoon at the lake, because for me it was a rare treat. The village beach was the only spot on the large lake where the public could swim, although it could hardly be called a beach because it was covered with rocks and grass and a few tall bushes. It did have a concrete dock that stuck out into the water where several wooden rowboats were tied up, a project of one of the village men who rented them out to fishermen. Two hundred feet out in the water someone had anchored a wooden raft that floated on four metal barrels, and this became the destination for us beginning swimmers.

We could walk out a long way before the water was over our heads, but if we ventured very far, it was icy cold, even in Dog Days, since it was fed by frigid springs on the deep bottom. We had heard that the lake had been carved out by the glacier many millenniums ago and was over a hundred feet deep in places, and I thought that part of the ancient ice was still sunk somewhere down there. Some townspeople claimed, with a straight face, that only a small part of the ice actually melted each spring, and the rest had merely sunk to the bottom.

A very old man lived in a shack by the beach, a village character called "Joe Indian". He claimed he didn't really know his age, but he was certain he was over a hundred. Some older residents in town said he had come from Canada in the early part of the century and distilled cedar oil on some of the little brooks in town. Back then, they said, he was "Joe Frenchman," but apparently some people thought it would be nice to have an Indian in town, so they gave him the name change, which he seemed to enjoy.

With a little imagination, you could say that Joe looked somewhat like an Indian, but my first glance at him when I was very young was disappointing. I saw no sign of the feathers or deerskin I'd expected. Instead he was wearing bib overalls and boots like most of the farmers. He got by with help from the overseer of the poor and the profits from his hobby of stealing bathing suits from clotheslines around the summer camps and renting them to kids who came to the beach without their own. None of the kids ever seemed worried about the possibility of acquiring a few germs or being convicted of wearing stolen property.

At home we welcomed any diversion that broke the monotony of haying and other summer jobs, so when a neighbor called to report that a group of cadets from Norwich University were riding their horses up a nearby road, several of us went to watch. We knew that the military college's cavalry unit frequently camped out in the back country to drill, scale cliffs, and shoot, but it was a surprise to hear that they were in our area. We waited and waited, thinking that they must have either stopped somewhere to rest or been engaged in a battle, but just as we were about to go home, one of our neighbors rode slowly by on his elderly gray work horse and appeared very bewildered to see the small crowd standing there and waving as he rode by. He was also completely unaware that several dozen mounted cadets were following only a few hundred feet behind. Everyone called him "General Washington" for the next few months.

Although the county fair was the biggest event of the summer, during August carnivals and small circuses came occasionally to nearby villages. Many of our neighbors went to the next town each summer to see a traveling show from New York State called the Chautauqua. It combined education with entertainment, and included puppets, plays, music, demonstrations, lectures, and musical numbers. The group of players traveled from town to town, and for about a week they gave a performance for the children every afternoon and another one for the entire family each evening.

I went only once, when I was eight years old, when my brother-in-law took his children and me one afternoon. The show took place in a big tent pitched in a field that was used for travelling shows and baseball games. The only act that I remember was a puppet show involving a rabbit family and I wondered for weeks how it was done, especially how Mrs. Rabbit could iron Peter's clothes while being manipulated by strings held by people above. The next day everyone said it was fortunate that we went in the afternoon, because that night a big wind blew down the tent, put out all the lights, and caused considerable confusion and a few bruised people. With some patching up of the tent and actors, however, the show went on as usual the following day.

It was always a relief when someone announced that Dog Days were probably over, even though it was a sign that frost and snow weren't far off. Nights had begun to cool, deer flies didn't bite as fiercely, the crickets stopped coming into the house, most of the scariest thunderstorms were over, and it was time once again to get ready for fall and the inevitable winter.

Chapter 11

The Time of Our Lives

"I set my watch every morning the instant I see Fred Turnbell's barn light come on." Oral Broadacres.

The clock and calendar dominated our lives. Most farmers, and even folks in town, felt it was important to rise with the sun. Stores opened at 7 o'clock to accommodate carpenters who might need something for their job that day and farmers who took their milk or cream to the creamery early. Garages, barber shops, mills, blacksmith shops, and other places of business were usually open at that time, too, and the road crew was always at work. If a farmer needed to drive to a nearby city for something special, he was thoroughly disgusted to find that he had to wait until the stores opened at nine o'clock to get his business done.

As the days became shorter in August, the earliest risers liked to keep an eye on their neighbors whose morning lights didn't come on until the disgraceful hour of six o'clock. These lazy lay-a-beds could expect no mercy when their name came up in discussions. No allowance was made for people with different internal time clocks, either. Dan Cooper married a girl he had met at agricultural school who could never cope with farm hours. Dan didn't mind that she preferred to do her work long after he had gone to bed, but it bothered the neighbors considerably, and for years she served as a bad example for other young girls.

There was a time for everything under the sun if we didn't waste it, we were all made to understand, and tardiness was not tolerated. Local doin's were planned so we could be there on time. Everything was geared to the schedules of the farmers since they and their families made up by far the largest percentage of the Vermont census. Evening events started at eight o'clock to give farmers a chance to milk their cows and get cleaned up. Church began at half-past ten and Sunday School was held after church, for the same reason. Schools started at 9 a.m. so the children would have time to get their morning barn chores done before walking to school. Each April a long school vacation was planned, both because mud season brought all traffic to a stop and because children were expected to help their families in their maple sugar operations at that time. Special events were seldom planned specifically for a Saturday because farmers and most other laborers worked on that day. Tuesday or Wednesday were as good as Saturday for an auction, town meeting, or Grange picnic. Sunday, between 9 and 4, was the only "official" day off, and many folks were in church for part of that time.

Although we were all expected to be prompt, hard-working, thrifty and honest, the working model for our predominantly Yankee community was a couple named Fred and Emma Turnbell. Emma epitomized those hard-working Vermont women who supposedly had the breakfast dishes done and all the beds made each morning before the rest of the family was up. I didn't like most of the models my family pointed out to me. "Why don't you get marks as good as Henry Peake's?" Or "Marcel LeDoux always gets the cows in on time even when his folks are away." Though I frequently pointed out that both Henry and Marcel had several less savory qualities that their parents never bragged about, it was of no avail, so my only recourse was to dislike them a bit more thoroughly. But when my mother and brothers mentioned that the Turnbells were the perfect examples of what we all should be, I found it difficult to disagree. One couldn't help but like them both. They didn't seem to have any annoying habits, and they were nice to everybody. Nevertheless, I decided to keep an eye on them on the theory that anyone who was reputed to be that perfect and disciplined must have some flaws.

Unlike many of our other old Yankee neighbors who looked to me as if a smile might fracture their faces, Fred and Emma smiled a lot and always had a nice word for everyone. They had come from quite different backgrounds. Fred was an old English Yankee whose ancestors had come to our town at the end of the Revolutionary War, but Emma's ancestors had arrived 40 years later, coming directly from Scotland. Her grandfather was born in Glasgow, and her father, Dwight MacDowell, was an Elder in the Presbyterian church. He seemed very old to me with his side whiskers and although he never wore kilts or carried a bagpipe, you could have guessed his nationality from 100 paces. Emma still had traces of the land of heather in her accent, too, and occasionally called a small child a "wee bairn". She said "mon" for man, and "aboot" for about and I learned that when she said "aye" it meant yes. She often ended a question with "eh?"

The Turnbells were not just on time, but ahead of time, always. Many people who are habitually late create balance in their lives by choosing spouses who are extra early, but Fred and Emma were exceptions and both were exceedingly prompt in everything they did. They painted their buildings before they started to peel, their roofs never leaked, and the spruce boughs for winter banking went around their house soon after Labor Day. Fred cut his woodpile at least a year ahead so it would be dry when they burned it. No bushes ever grew on their roadsides since he scythed them before they were barely visible, and his farm manure was spread soon after the snow melted in the spring. We knew that every bill in the Turnbell household was paid a few days before it was due, and we weren't surprised to learn that they ordered their fertilizer a full year before they actually needed it.

Emma and Fred were early risers. Though "up at five" was the rule in our neighborhood, they always rose at four, and it had to be a special occasion if they stayed up beyond eight o'clock at night. People who knew Emma well said that she always tore off the calendar two or three days before the month was over, and after we began to have Daylight Savings Time, she set the clocks an hour ahead on the Wednesday before it began on Sunday. The Turnbells were the only people we knew who seemed to like the change to the new fangled idea. Most farmers sputtered endlessly about "the gol ram government messing with God's time," and some folks refused to change their clocks on the premise that Daylight Savings Time meant only that everyone would lose an hour of sleep every day all summer. Certainly no respectable Yankee could ever quit work and bed down while it was still daylight.

At holidays the Turnbell's efficiency was particularly exasperating to the rest of us. When we took our flowers to the cemetery on Memorial Day, we were not surprised to see that the bouquets of lilacs on the Turnbell family lot were already beginning to fade. Each year they cut their Christmas tree before it snowed, stored it in a shed, and took it snowless into the house in early December. On Christmas night they stripped off all the decorations and by bedtime they had labeled the boxes and stored them in the attic for the following December. The next morning any passer-by could see their tree perched in a snowbank on the lawn for the chickadees to play in for the rest of the winter.

Fred invariably started haying the middle of June, though most farmers felt the weather was never good enough for haying until after Independence Day. We could be sure that they would be completely finished in time to attend the county fair in mid-August, even during a rainy year. My friend, Roger, went with them to the fair one year, and said that they arrived at the grounds by eight a.m., just as the gates opened. They made a speedy tour of the cattle and horse barns, checked out the craft exhibits, and wandered through the Midway where they stopped to eat an early lunch at the Grange food booth. Then they watched part of the stage show and a few horse races. Rob was disappointed that they never saw the big parade of cattle and farm machinery around the race track in late afternoon, however, because nothing could hinder Fred from being "ta home" in time to start the evening chores at half past four, just as his cows expected. The Coomers' poor cows, on the other hand, never had a chance to enjoy any such schedule, since the boys milked them whenever they got around to it. Never governed by a clock or calendar, the three boys and their father spent all three days at the fair and wouldn't have dreamed of missing the fireworks.

Though I looked for a superior attitude in the Turnbells and the snobbery one would expect to go with their high standards, Emma and Fred had none. They never discussed, at least in public, the sloppy habits of us less efficient folks. They didn't even criticize the Coomers, who served as models for what we should not be and ran their farm exactly opposite from the way the Turnbells ran theirs. The Coomers always finished haying during an October snowstorm, cut their wood as they burned it, and patched their roof during a rainstorm if they did it at all. They put on their double windows the week before Christmas or later, the same windows they had taken off on the Fourth of July. The family was always late for funerals, auctions, and town meeting, even though they lived only a half mile from the village, and they seldom spent much time cleaning themselves up before going. By contrast, the Turnbells, whose farm was four miles back in the country, were always a half hour early for everything, even on a snowy day. Often they got to a funeral before the corpse.

The only fault I ever found, and my family would never admit it, was that the Turnbells' efficiency sometimes led to small disasters. Each year they planted their tomato seeds near the kitchen stove on Lincoln's birthday instead of waiting until the proper time, Town Meeting Day, the first Tuesday of March. Everyone admired the beautiful, budded, two-foot plants growing in their bay window on Mothers' Day, but Fred couldn't resist setting them out in the garden as soon as the daffodils bloomed, instead of waiting to plant them ten frost-free days after Memorial Day. Consequently, their plants nearly always froze on the first June night that the moon was full, and Fred had to drive to the hardware store, buy some much smaller ones, and set them out at the proper time.

Since Fred couldn't bear not to harvest his garden early, either, his potatoes always went into the cellar for winter storage when the weather was still warm, in late August. Consequently, they often rotted before winter was over. We heard that he always picked his apples before they were quite ripe, which made his cider far too sour to enjoy. Every spring he scattered the buckets in his maple woods early, just before an unexpected late spring storm buried them deep in snow. But even though he had to search for them beneath the snow, he invariably made the first batch of maple syrup in town. Since the tap holes in his trees usually dried up before the last run of sap, however, most years his syrup production was no greater than anyone else's. I liked to point out to my family that because they invariably took off their storm windows the first warm April day, they had to shiver in their home for the next three weeks. My family members were not impressed. In their book, few things were more important than doing things on time, or a bit earlier.

It was a sad day when I, along with most of the town, went to Fred's funeral. The minister spent most of the service discussing the tragedy "we never could possibly understand." But we did understand. Fred was 75 and had sold his farm to a nephew a few months before. He was aware that he was getting along in years and had no intention of becoming a burden to anybody. He had accomplished all he felt the Lord expected, and seen everything he wanted to see. Once he had taken a train excursion to Burlington, ventured a few miles into Canada twice, and one year had crossed the Connecticut River into New Hampshire to visit a cousin. Since all his life he had never made anyone wait, there was no point in making his Maker wait, either. After discussing everything fully with Emma, he had gone to the barn one day and drunk a bottle of horse liniment, plainly marked "For External Use Only."

Three months after Fred's death, Emma found she had cancer, and in her calm and quiet way she prepared for her own death, which came within a short time. The couple were so perfectly matched in all their efficient ways, that on the day of her funeral everyone realized that she had probably willed it to happen in precisely that way. She just couldn't keep Fred waiting.

Emma's was a moving service, but wholly inadequate because the new preacher knew almost nothing about the couple. He repeated the familiar passages, and once more sadly pointed out that only God understood why such things come to pass. When, at the end of the final prayer he referred to Emma as the "late Mrs. Turnbell", my brother gave me a nudge. Everyone there knew that he couldn't have been more wrong.

154

Chapter 12

Saturday Night

"I don't come to town none too often, but when I do, it's Rowdy-dow!" Pete Roundhouse, shouting in the street on one of his Sa'day night toots.

Saturday night was just another night of the week in our little hamlet, but it was *the* night in the considerably larger village next to ours which everyone called "Town". Even though the two stores in our village stayed open until eight o'clock on Saturday night, many folks went to shop in Town, where the action was. A six day work week meant that payday was on Saturday, so that was the night to go out and make whoopee.

Town was the trading center for the populations of several mountain communities surrounding it. Unlike ours, it was a "wet" town, which meant that the voters there had approved the sale of alcoholic beverages. Consequently, it supported five beer parlors and three taverns, some of which were also restaurants. For additional entertainment there were two pool rooms, a movie house, a dance hall, and even a private gym that sometimes offered amateur boxing matches where local farm youths and granite workers held bouts. Several stores and a barber shop were always busy on Saturday night, as well.

During daylight hours, Town supplied many services that were not available in our village. These included a bank, a print shop which published the weekly newspaper, several garages, a small hospital, and you could find a doctor, dentist, lawyer, and photographer there, too. Some small industries flourished, including a foundry-machine shop that made furnaces and manure spreaders. But the main source of outside income for the village was the processing of large chunks of granite that had been cut or blasted out of quarries on a nearby mountain. These were moved by train to several long sheds scattered around the village, where the blocks were cut and polished. Although some shops made cemetery monuments, most of the granite was machined into large chunks that were used in the construction of public buildings around the country. The heavy granite that left the area by trucks and train brought badly needed cash into the otherwise depressed area.

The granite workers, who were predominantly Italian and French-Canadian, got good wages, and unlike the frugal Scots and Yankees, they were free-spenders who liked to enjoy life. Their attitude greatly helped the stores, taverns and other businesses about town to flourish, but there was a sad reason for their seeming zest for living. The stone cutters knew that their lives would be greatly shortened by the granite dust they inhaled in the unventilated sheds, so many developed a devil-may-care attitude and led lively, rough and rowdy lives. The upshot was that Town became known as "Little Chicago" with a state-wide reputation as a hard-drinking, hard-living, frontier community. It was an exciting place for a naive farm boy to visit on a Saturday night.

The folks who didn't have farm chores went to Town early, in the late afternoon. They got first crack at the limited parking spots, causing folks like us, who came after chores, to walk a quarter mile or so to get into the center of town. The summer of my first trip. I went with my brother, and as we drew nearer there was a carnival atmosphere on the streets. Crowds of people filled the sidewalks and men greeted each other loudly across the street, sometimes with obscenities. Everybody seemed to be having a good time, at least early in the evening before several fights broke out. Since my brother wanted to join his friends, I was free to wander about town.

I didn't have time to go to the movies that night because my brother wanted to get home before the double feature would be finished. But I didn't really mind because the free show on the street and sidewalks was pretty interesting. Like the fair, Saturday night brought out people who never appeared at any other time and apparently they came from far back in the hills. Many had a quite different Yankee accent than the one I was accustomed to hearing, and a few were probably mentally disturbed, although it was hard to tell for sure since it seemed to me that a lot of people who were usually normal were also acting a bit wild. For some, Town seemed to be a place worth dressing up for, because they looked as if they were headed for church. But others had obviously come directly from the barn, shop, or woods, and they smelled accordingly. Some men had week-old beards and others looked as if they cut their own hair, but only occasionally.

Some people had brought items to sell or trade, and others returned empty beer or soda pop bottles to the stores. A lot of women were obviously pregnant and some of the same women were also carrying a child in their arms and had two or three others trailing them. Large women in colorful print dresses gathered on the sidewalk chatting with each other, sometimes in French or Italian, while their children pleaded incessantly to go to the picture show. I didn't know most of them, but it was easy to pick out members of some of the larger clans by the way they resembled each other. While the women talked and shopped, most of their men retreated to the drinking places or pool halls.

I peeked into the barber shop and was surprised to see four barbers at work, many shelves of shaving mugs on the shelves, and every seat around the perimeter filled with waiting customers. I had heard that most businessmen in larger towns went to the barbershop each morning to be shaved with their own brush and mug, and this scene seemed to confirm that tale. The men, according to the reports, then went to one of the eating places for breakfast, read their newspapers, and swapped news with each other before they went to work at nine. I figured that by then most of the farmers had already been at work for 4 hours.

Each drinking place along the main street was apparently full, although by looking in the windows it was hard to tell because the tobacco smoke was so thick I could barely see past the first three booths. When I first walked by, the customers seemed to be having a good time talking and laughing, but when I peered in later, most of them looked forlorn and dejected and were staring silently into their drinks. The tough-looking, brightly painted waitresses, many well past middle age but trying desperately to look young, were busy refilling their customers' glass mugs.

Young men with cars cruised back and forth along the main street, hoping to pick up a girl or, if that failed, to find some male friends to spend the evening with. Those without cars and money hung out with friends on the street, sometimes sharing a drink or smoke with those who were old enough or had cash enough to supply them.

As I strolled along I met Mike Jones, a school friend, who told me that some men were on the lookout for the brightly painted girls and women who supplemented their income by prowling the sidewalks. "They always disappear early in the evening, but they'll come back after 10 o'clock when another batch of clients will be looking for them," he said. We overheard one man tell his friend that visiting one of the women once a month kept him healthy, but none of them looked like a very tempting health treatment to me.

Although that night I was satisfied with walking back and forth and looking at the people, on my rare subsequent trips, if I had the 20 cents admission price, I went to the movies with a friend. The first show at the Idle Hour Theatre was at seven o'clock and was always packed with people, even though they seldom showed anything on Saturday nights except a Gene Autry or Roy Rogers Western, along with an even cheaper detective film, such as The Fat Man. Because of chores, most of us farm kids got to the movie house after the first show was already in progress, so we sat through what was left of that film, watched the second feature from beginning to end, and stayed into the second running of the first long enough to catch up on what we had missed. Sometimes they showed a cartoon or a newsreel, too, although these were rare on weekends when there was a double feature. Though Saturday night films were usually predictable and junky, I enjoyed them tremendously because I went so rarely. After a thrilling runaway stagecoach and a few shoot-em-ups, even the lively streets outside the theater seemed pretty quiet.

The newsreels were exciting, even though they were at least six months old before they arrived at the theater. It was a novelty to actually see up on the big screen the people we had only read or heard about before. The golden voice of Lowell Thomas and massive background music could have made even a film about lawn mowing exciting, but the newsreels featured such events as the second inauguration of Franklin Roosevelt, the young Dionne Quints, new airships taking off, and other exciting news that had filled the newspapers long before.

After the first film we could count on a preview of the movies the theater would be showing throughout the upcoming week. These were Hollywood's better films and quite different from the Saturday night specials. I wanted to see all of them, but unless it was *Gone With the Wind,* or *The Wizard of Oz,* never did. The theater showed one movie twice on both Monday and Tuesday nights, a different one on Wednesday and Thursday, and the cheapies on Friday and Saturday. There were never any shows on Sunday, and a film was seldom held over, no matter how popular it was. If folks wanted to see a highly advertised film such as *Mutiny on the Bounty*, they had to get there long before it started or they wouldn't get a seat.

The man who owned the theater was very strict and selected his films carefully, with the morality of his patrons in mind, an anomaly in such an unruly town. He never posted advertising posters showing kissing or scantily clad women in front of his theater or in the lobby, and he allowed no food nor drink inside. We all knew that if we talked or fooled around when the film was on, he would be there within a few seconds, telling us we must either straighten out immediately, or leave. The theater had a small balcony which was usually taken over by young couples, and he watched these especially carefully for any signs of monkey business.

He showed no movies with even a suggestion of actual sex, and once, we heard, he stopped the reel when a woman on the screen mentioned she was going to have a baby. He immediately apologized to the theatergoers, refunded everyone's money, and sent them on their way. It seemed to me a pretty mild statement compared to the things I'd heard mentioned on the street outside the theater on a Saturday night, but Mr. Carr had his standards. I don't know how he ever allowed Clark Gable to announce in 1940 that he "didn't give a damn," but the night I saw *"Gone With the Wind"* there was an audible gasp from the audience at that statement. None of us were prepared for such language from the screen at the Idle Hour.

In spite of his upstanding morality, Mr. Carr was not apparently up-to-date on politics. Bumper stickers were very new, and one night a camper from the lake who had a "Norman Thomas" sticker on his car, parked it in the wrong spot. Mr. Carr broke into the sound track of the movie, and over the microphone politely told Mr. Norman Thomas to please go out and move his car. Most people paid little attention, having no idea who the famous Socialist running for president was, but the campers enjoyed the joke for years.

Since Town's reputation was widespread, it became a favorite target of revivalist preachers who hoped to change the aberrant ways of its citizens. On some Saturday evenings in summer, a man stood on a wooden box at one of the street corners urging that the listeners attend an upcoming revival meeting, which might be their last chance to repent and be saved before the imminent end of the world. These preachers always attracted a small group of people, some of them very drunk. Each Saturday a few converts decided to mend their ways and seek a better way of life, and we heard that their conversions sometimes lasted almost until the following Saturday night.

Occasionally a Salvation Army band of five or six men and women with cymbals, trumpets and a big drum appeared. They collected a large group of listeners as their lively gospel music floated over the fallen angels on a balmy summer night. The band wore blue uniforms which showed signs of wear, but one had to admire their dedication to what must have seemed like a discouraging mission, as they watched the merrymakers and drunkards stagger by.

Bill Colby, our neighbor's hired man who didn't have a car, sometimes asked my brother for a ride to Town. He always said "I just live all week for Saturday night," although it didn't seem too likely that he would remember much of it. He always warned us to be sure to take him home with us when we left, even though he admitted he probably wouldn't want to go. "I'll be at the first table in Brunos's tavern," he said, "But if you don't see me sittin' there, look under it."

160

Bill was right. He never did want to leave, even when the bars were closing at midnight. Sometimes I saw him on the sidewalks before he went into Bruno's, a lighted cigarette in both hands and a bottle under each arm, talking happily with his cronies. He always took his paycheck with him, and after playing the juke box, buying his week's supply of smokes, and treating friends, he invariably returned home completely broke. Knowing this would happen, he gave us a small tip on the way to Town to pay for delivering him back home. His boss told us that he always needed an advance in pay whenever he needed a new barn frock or a pair of overalls.

On Saturday night, Town was the closest thing to a real frontier town I ever hoped to see, but, even though there were often fights and lots of yelling, I never heard of any murders or other serious crime. During hunting season some men carried rifles in their cars and trucks, and sometimes I saw a knife and revolver sticking out from beneath a red plaid jacket, but apparently they were meant only for deer. One bar had a sign forbidding any weapons inside, but apparently most establishments didn't care.

Fist fights were almost as frequent between women as men. We sometimes had to walk out into the street to get around two women on the sidewalk who were swearing, screaming, slugging, pulling hair and kicking each other. These fights always attracted a lot of onlookers but nobody apparently ever tried to stop them, and just stood by enjoying the show. I never felt like sticking around because fights sometimes had a way of spreading rapidly, so I never found out how they came out, but I don't know how they could have avoided a few knocked-out teeth and broken noses. Many of the jokes often repeated about Town concerned the shortage of teeth among its inhabitants.

Occasionally we had to step over men lying on the sidewalk who had either been knocked down in a fight or had simply fallen from too much bottled merriment. I was quite concerned the first time I saw one, but nobody else seemed to be upset or excited enough to call a doctor or ambulance. The local newspaper never mentioned any of the ruckus, so such events seemed to be merely "business as usual." The local jail held only

161

two cells, which, if they were ever used at all, were probably filled early.

Apparently no one felt the need of any more law and order than they already had. I often heard people mention that there was a policeman in Town, but I never saw him on the street. One boy told me that he was an older man who prudently always found some excuse to disappear early on Saturday night, probably to avoid any situation where he would be outnumbered. Since there were no state police, each county was protected by a sheriff who looked after a dozen or more towns. But the sheriff was usually elderly, too, and his main functions seemed to be to serve papers, be present when court was in session, and take bad kids to reform school. Each town also elected a town constable who usually collected taxes and sometimes checked out local dances for signs of mischief. The people in Town were apparently expected to take care of problems in their own way, and we would occasionally see the door of a drinking place suddenly fly open as the burley bartender tossed an unruly patron outside.

The high point of each Saturday evening happened when someone yelled, "Here comes the Queen of the Mountain!" A few minutes later a team of work horses, one large and one small, rattled along the street pulling a long wooden farm wagon. Perched high on a seat, driving the team, was a middle-aged woman wearing a brown toque and smoking a cigar as she waved to the delighted crowd and flashed a toothless smile. I don't know where the Queen parked her vehicle and steeds, but she soon appeared on the sidewalk carrying an armful of empty beer bottles to redeem. I heard that many campers at the lake went to Town on Saturday night especially to see her, and she probably furnished a lot of material for winter discussions as city folks related how they spent their summer in the country.

Even if I couldn't stay until midnight, I heard many stories about the goings on when, as the law prescribed, the bars closed and customers staggered out. That was apparently a good time to be out of the way because even if the drunks couldn't walk well, many thought they could still fight. Apparently a favorite way to start a scrap was to yell a few insults and obscenities to people, whether they knew them or not. Far too many of these characters thought that they were perfectly able to drive home, too, and the more sober folks considered it prudent to get away before too many had located their cars and figured out how to start them.

The people in our neighborhood who most enjoyed Saturday night were the single hired men and woodsmen who had no wives to keep them in line. The story circulated among our neighbors that on one Monday morning, a man reported to work somewhat scarred up and bruised. Under questioning, he related that he had come home from Town somewhat late and had "one hell of a time getting up the stairs." He finally made it, he said "but the gol ram bed was racing round and round the room. Well, I took after it, but after a couple of laps, I seen that I weren't about to overtake it. So I said, 'gol dern ye, I'll wait by the door, and when you come round, I'll mount you.' Well, I stood there by the door, and when the bed came racing by, I gave one hang of a leap, and, by gory, I missed it!" It was a widely reported story, but most people thought his scars had undoubtedly resulted from a weekend Town brawl.

Although I often heard Town discussed, few people ever suggested it needed cleaning up. Our neighbors thought that if there had to be those kinds of things going on, it was a good idea to have it confined in one place, and at least a few miles away from our village. Town was also useful as a bad example for other hamlets. My brother once asked Larry LaPoint, a regular visitor, how he could carouse so wildly on Saturday night, and then show up at Mass the next morning looking so pious. Larry promptly replied, "Imagine how I might act down there if I weren't a good church goer!"

After each Saturday night visit to Town, I thought about the place for many weeks afterward. It provided an insight into a way of life that was completely different from that in our little town only 6 miles away. I still wonder whatever happened to the Mountain Queen.

Chapter 13

The County Fair

"I shore enjoy seeing the collection of weird folks that show up at the fair each year. I wish they wouldn't stare at me so cussed much, though." Friday Minot.

Everybody in our neighborhood went to the county fair each year unless he was on his death bed. It was by far the biggest event of the summer and, like every youngster, I had wanted to go since I was old enough to learn where everyone went that day in late August-the only summer day my brothers rushed through the milking and abandoned all other unnecessary work.

The year I was 13 was my third year at the fair, and by then I knew pretty much what to expect. Since I was finally old enough to run around by myself, I looked forward to it. But it could never compare to that first year, the year I was eleven, when my mother determined that I was finally old enough to go with my older brother, his wife, and my older sister, all of whom were expected to keep an eye on me. We went on Thursday, the first day, when kids got in free, which was also the traditional fair day for farm families to go. We would miss seeing Friday's big cavalcade of cattle, horses, and farm machinery around the race track, and hearing the politicians who came on Governor's Day, but it was a good time to meet the neighbors and friends we hadn't seen all summer and exchange local gossip. If the weather was good, the crowds were largest that day because the pessimistic Yankees worried it might rain the other two days.

My anticipation grew as the day came near. The day before I helped my brothers check the farm fences. Everyone knew that if cows ever broke out and ate up our garden or a neighbor's, it would be on fair day when everyone was gone. Thursday morning finally arrived, hot and steamy. After finishing my chores of feeding the chickens and calves, and wolfing down a big bowl of oatmeal and several graham rolls, I dressed in my school clothes and good shoes, which seemed slightly tight after several weeks of going barefoot.

My sister and I got into the back seat of my brother's car, headed for what I was sure would be the most exciting adventure of my life. In the Model A Ford with its horn that squawked "oodle", we bumped down the hill to the main road which was also unpaved, washboard-like, and filled with potholes, just like our back road. A few miles up that road we dipped down into a narrow valley with high hills on both sides, a spot my family always called 'Dry Pond,' although it had been officially christened 'Runaway Pond.' We passed a good-sized granite marker, placed there in 1910, a century after the 100 foot deep Long Pond had broken loose on its north end and completely emptied into the valley beyond. To have witnessed this amazing flood on a beautiful June day must have been awesome, and I wished I could have been there to see it, safely perched on high ground, of course.

After about 10 miles we stopped at the Busy Bee roadside stand for gasoline. Nearby was a little zoo filled with animals in cages, including a woodchuck, raccoon, turtle, wild rabbit, monkey, a very sleepy owl, and, most exciting of all, a big black bear named Queenie. She looked immense and dangerous, but she was accustomed to people and lived well from all the food visitors gave her. A large sign hung over her pen: "Watch this bear drink pop. 5 cents." Because a big crowd stopped on fair days, Queenie got a huge amount of the soda pop she loved. My sister and I watched a visitor hand her a bottle. She took it in both paws, stood up tall, threw back her head, and drank it, just as a person would.

I could have watch Queenie all day, but the gas tank was filled and we were soon on our way in a long line of cars headed for the fairground. Most were closed vehicles, but there were a few Model T Fords and one flashy car with the top folded down which my brother said was a roadster. The big Packard in front of us was especially fascinating because, curiously, all of its Isinglass curtains were in place in spite of the hot day. We wondered what was going on in there that could be such a secret, but couldn't get a glimpse of the inhabitants. Even from a distance the fair was exciting. I hung out the window to get a better glimpse of the tall Ferris wheel, the whirling merry-go-round, and many giant tents with flags flying from the tops. The huge grandstand had a sloping roof completely covered with a large painted arrow directing small planes to the nearest airport in St. Johnsbury.

When we got nearer the grounds we could hear the lively music of the merry-go-round blaring out "A Bicycle Built for Two," "The Sidewalks of New York" and "Battle Hymn of the Republic." As the touring car with the Isinglass curtains turned left into the road that led to the fairgrounds, several male hands stuck out from both sides of the car to signal. At the ticket booth, however, a small, dainty female hand came out to hand over the money for the admission. I hoped to get a good look at the people inside the Packard when they disembarked, but we lost them as men with flat straw hats and colored canes directed us to different parking areas.

When it was our turn to enter, my brother handed over the tickets he had bought in advance at our local store, and we headed toward the oval race track. A man with a badge and a stiff, colorful whip closed the gates on the road crossing the track. A few horses trotted by and then he opened the gate and waved us across to the oval interior, where more men with canes directed us to park in double lines amongst more cars than I ever knew were in this world.

Beyond the parking area a group of men were playing baseball, and a small crowd had collected around them. They had on striped uniforms and knickers, just like the ones we'd seen Babe Ruth wear in the newspapers. My brother said that lots of towns had baseball teams and some of the nearby furniture factories and fire departments did, as well. Beyond the baseball game we could see a collection of tents, and near them some brown-uniformed Boy Scouts were practicing signaling with wigwag flags. Other Scouts were building a tower out of posts, and still others were making a campfire. I was very curious about them, but my brother preferred to inspect the cattle, sheep, and horse barns and felt I shouldn't go off on my own.

My sister, who had been to the fair before, wanted to go immediately to the Midway instead of the barns. We can see cows any day at home," she protested. But my brother wanted her to look after me. As we neared the barns, we were greeted with the familiar smell of farm animals, an instant, unpleasant reminder of chore time at home. I forgot about the Scouts and the Midway as soon as I saw the strange animals-Dutch Belted and Brown Swiss dairy cows, huge Hereford and Black Angus beef cattle, and even one Brahma bull. Since we had only black and white Holsteins on our farm, and no one raised oxen, sheep, or goats in our town, they were a novelty. The weird poultry breeds didn't resemble any of our chickens, either.

Near the barns, in a ring encircled with ropes attached to posts, nervous 4-H boys and girls were parading their livestock before the judges, hoping to win ribbons and prize money. The cattle and sheep had all been recently washed, and their hoofs and horns polished. One small heifer, just as it reached the ring, suddenly decided to lie down, while its young owner stood by helplessly and began to cry. Behind the barns, several riders exercised their horses. Some were obviously farm boys having fun, but others were older and seemed very serious, probably hoping to win ribbons and have their pictures taken with their spirited palominos for the local paper. These men wore cowboy hats, embroidered shirts, boots with large spurs, and some had holstered guns attached to wide cartridge belts. Most had lariats hanging from their saddles which were decorated with silver buckles and colorful glass stones.

A short distance from the other riders, several slim young women with bright red lips were slowly riding sleek horses round and round in small circles. They looked like pictures I'd seen of people dressed for a fox hunt, with tight breeches, dark blue jackets, and derby hats, and every one of them looked alike. The girls sat very straight on small saddles without horns or lariats and someone behind us said they were riding 'English' rather than 'Western' style.

A dozen old men sat on bales of straw beside one of the horse barns, chewing tobacco or smoking cigars, apparently not intending to move from their spots until the fair was over. Some were toothless, most had long, gray hair and a few had beards. My brother stopped to talk with some of the former horse dealers he recognized, and I stood on one foot and then the other, listening as they all bragged endlessly about horses they used to own and the clever trades they had orchestrated. Some seemed to be swapping small items with each other, such as jackknifes and watches.

Finally we moved along, but inside the barns the conversation was just as boring. The owners of the cattle were eager to show them off and they pointed to the boards over their stalls covered with dozens of ribbons they had won at the many fairs they had previously toured. Each knew the complete history of his cows and the ribbons they'd won, and seemed more than willing to share their knowledge with anyone they could stop. One farmer was ready to keep us there all day, I thought, as he complained about how much better his critters behaved in the show ring than those of his competitors. "The others won," he said bitterly, "only because the judge showed favorites."

Some other men, who apparently stayed in the barn with their cattle all day, were complaining loudly about how the government was to blame for the sad state of farming, the problems of getting good help, and the behavior of the young men who didn't want to stay on the farm. I spotted several little beds the farmers had made up in some empty stalls and figured that they had to spend all three days and nights there with their animals. I didn't envy the young 4-Hers and FFA boys who had to milk their cows and feed and water them for all that time in a strange place. Finally we completed our tour and followed my brother outside the barns. The outdoors reeked with the familiar smell of manure, too, but the added aroma of cigar smoke, shredded straw, and burning gasoline made it seem less like our farm, and it was pleasantly intermingled with the fragrance of hamburgers and hot dogs cooking on a gas grill in a nearby eating booth.

After a brief walk around the machinery tents to see the tractors, hay loaders, new-fangled milking machines, and modern cars with radios, we headed at last toward the Midway. The noise level rose as we got closer, nearly drowning out the music of the carousel. The carnies, as I learned the carnival workers were called, yelled loudly to lure people into their shows, play their games, or to take a chance on a raffle. They looked far different from the Yankees I was accustomed to seeing, and I stared at them as we walked past. I figured they must have got their jobs because of their loud voices which they exercised without stopping. One shrill-voiced woman cried, "Walter Baker's new milk chocolate bars- three five-cent bars for ten cents," over and over. The words were to ring in my head for days.

Crowds of people milled in both directions past the booths lining the midway. The opportunities for spending money there were endless. Hawkers offered chances to throw baseballs at wooden milk bottles, shoot a real rifle, pitch pennies, knock stuffed animals off a shelf, throw darts, or play roulette. If we won, we could take home all sorts of stuffed toys. Others offered, for a dime, to guess our weight, and we'd win a cigar if they were wrong by more than 5 pounds. For a bit more money we could see a magic show, learn the secrets of sex, or find out how the world would end. I wasn't tempted to try my luck at winning a painted doll, by betting which hole the rat on the big wheel would dive into, or by buying a ticket on an Indian blanket, because I had decided in advance that I would spend my thirty cents only on the thrilling rides at the far end of the Midway.

I lingered a bit longer beside the little stands that sold cameras, knives, field glasses, and other cheap treasures, and was especially intrigued with the one filled with Dick Tracy handcuffs, badges, and cap guns. Another booth featured Amelia Earhart helmets and Tom Mix belts, complete with dummy cartridges and holsters. I walked more quickly past the less interesting booths that displayed dangling toys that people were buying to hang in their cars-large dice, monkeys, little birds, and similar items.

A big tent was packed with players beneath a sign that said "Bingo." Many women, with a smattering of men, sat on benches huddled over long tables as the announcer shouted "B 14" or "G 47" in an excited tone. Whenever anyone yelled

170

"Bingo," he said, "Now, don't disturb your cards, this player may be wrong." At one end of the tent was a shelf covered with clocks, toasters, stuffed bears, lamps, mirrors, and more. Many of our neighbors always played there, my sister said, and occasionally won something. The game appeared honest but a man standing beside us warned his companion that the year before he'd noticed that the people carrying off the biggest prizes were always part of the carny brotherhood.

We passed two Gypsy women in bright-colored dresses, gold earrings, and kerchiefs, telling fortunes by gazing at their client's hand. A bit later we overheard one man tell another that all the while he was having his fortune told, the Gypsy was trying to get her other hand into his pocket. I wondered if those were some of the Gypsies that had camped in our town two weeks ago.

We stopped for awhile near a tall pole where one could win a cigar by pounding a platform with a hammer that sent a weight upward to ring a bell at the top. A group of boys and young men had gathered, wanting to prove their prowess to their girl friends or each other. The pole was marked into different categories such as 'Weakling', 'Big boy', 'Sort-of-hero', and 'Powerman'. If you hit it just right, the bell would ring, and when it didn't, some of the burly, tattoo-covered men in tee-shirts looked pretty embarrassed. Harvey White, who was standing next to us, said that he saw the man in charge adjust the machine to make it harder to ring when he was losing too many cheap cigars, so he figured that he probably made it easier to ring when he needed more business. Some of the boys who hit the bell smoked their first cigars that day, and it was easy to spot them by their loud coughing and pale greenish complexions.

It took a while to get past all the sideshows and their enticing signs. One promised that for only a dime we could watch a wild man from Borneo tear live chickens apart and eat them, feathers and all. For other dimes one could view either the world's fattest woman, biggest pig, strongest man, or a two-headed calf. We noticed that most folks who went into the sideshows looked ashamed at being duped and didn't mention it later. But Effie Greene was felt differently. She didn't like being deceived, and when she came out she didn't mind telling everyone within hearing distance that the two-headed calf was stuffed, with the extra head sewed on. She also said she heard that the fat lady was not nearly as large as she looked on the poster in front, and neither was the giant pig, which was also stuffed. Her brother, who had paid fifteen cents to see people walking over hot coals and jagged glass, had told her, she announced, that they appeared to have a safe path through the hazardous materials.

I stopped, wide-eyed, in front of a platform where two brightly painted, scantily clad girls were wiggling around to the beat of a small drum played by a scruffy-looking, young bearded man. The barker promised that, if we were 21, the girls would reveal everything for us, once we'd shelled out a quarter. We looked around at the crowd and saw a line had formed, waiting for the show to start. Most of them were grinning, toothless, old duffers, but a few were younger men who looked rather sheepish. One older man from our town emerged from the booth later and announced in a loud voice, "Now I've seen the fair, and I'm a goin' home."

Later in the day, I ran into Mike, one of my schoolmates, who said that he had been very proud to get into the girlie show at age 13 with his last quarter. But all the girls did was shake their bodies and dance around a little. Then, he complained, the barker asked for another twenty-five cents to see the "main" show that he had promised outside. Mike missed out on that for lack of another quarter. I was beginning to wise up about carnival life.

As we made our way through the crowd on the Midway we kept meeting neighbors and other folks we knew, but also throngs of strangers, the like of which I'd never imagined. Girls covered with tattoos and grown men in shorts passed by. Many young couples, obviously not Yankees, shamelessly hugged each other, not caring who saw them. I stared after some dwarfs and pointed out to my sister the first black women I had ever seen. A group of girls with brightly painted faces nearly bumped into us. Some, I noticed, had hair dyed a bright red, and one was completely bald. Motorcyclists wearing black leather caps and vests jostled past us as did numerous policemen, and I encountered my first blind people, a one- legged man, and folks speaking strange languages.

It seemed likely to me that a lot of people had crawled out of a sick bed to be there that day, including a man with a wooden leg that looked as if it had been cut off a table, women in wheelchairs, folks on crutches, and some hobbling feebly with canes. Numerous drunks staggered around and some other men looked as if they might have been let out of jail for the day. I kept looking for the pickpockets my family had warned us about but they must have been skillful because I never saw any. Later that day, though, I saw one man searching frantically through his pockets for a wallet that was obviously no longer there, so apparently they had been busy.

I still hadn't seen anything that would make me part with my precious thirty cents. The games were fun to watch, but it took only a few minutes of watching to figure out that the claw machines picking up quarters and jewelry inevitably dropped them just before reaching the door, and the "wheels of fortune" usually stopped a bit too suddenly to be pure luck. We must have been among the few suspicious onlookers, because there was no shortage of players. Many hired men and mill hands saved their cash all summer for their one big day at the fair.

As I was lingering beside a roulette game, trying to figure it out, Henry Parks, a young farmer who lived a few miles from us, turned away from the booth looking dazed. My brother whispered that it looked like he had lost his summer savings at the first place he had come to. A bit later another young man we knew slightly rushed around frantically trying to borrow two dollars so he could continue playing a dice game the carney had assured him he would certainly win in "just one more try."

I was ready to go for the rides that were now in sight, but the grownups wanted to see the Floral Hall and Grange and 4-H buildings, I suppose on the off-chance we might learn something there. The Floral Hall was a long building lined on each side with exhibits, crafts, and people selling things. The quiet there was a welcome change from the noisy Midway, and I had to admit there was plenty to see. Among the interesting displays were exhibits by local stores of the newest refrigerators, milk coolers, and radios for all those lucky folks who had electricity on their farms. I thought the display of stuffed native wild animals by the State Fish and Game Department was very interesting, especially the two little bears that were paddling a canoe. For a long time we watched a man doing magic tricks to attract a crowd for his plumbing demonstration, and I could hardly wait to try them out at home.

From there we went to the building that held the arts and crafts and 4-H exhibits of handiwork, flowers, and garden produce. I hurried by the fancy embroidery, quilts and paintings, all sporting red, white, or blue ribbons they had won, but stopped and examined carefully the display of giant vegetables. I wondered if I might not be able to win some of the 20 cent prize money the following year. Our cold hilltop made it difficult to get vegetables to grow to a large size in time to take to the fair, but it would be worth trying. I could think of several things to do with the prize money.

At long last, we reached the rides at the far end of the fairgrounds. The Ferris wheel seemed a lot higher than it had looked from a distance, but the merry-go-round seemed safe enough. The Tilt-a-whirl was filled with young girls screaming as they were snapped around in spinning tubs that spun around a bumpy track. A fourth ride, the swings, was spinning the riders far outward, over the crowd.

My sister decided that the Ferris wheel should be our first choice, and I reckoned it would be well worth 10 cents. As we approached, I had some misgivings because it was very high, and the engine extremely noisy, but I had never heard of one breaking, so I let my sister push me into line. We paid our dimes and sat gingerly in the swaying seat while the attendant, a bored, dark-complexioned man, fastened us in with a bar across the front of the seat. Our seat jerked ahead as he loaded the next couple. Then it started rolling, and I held my breath and clenched the bar as it went higher and higher, then dipped and went down and up around again. I bravely kept my eyes open the second time around, but my stomach felt queasy. After several turns the wheel suddenly stopped, with us right at the top, and the seat swung back and forth in a frightening way. After I caught my breath, I saw a view I thought I'd never forget-the entire fairgrounds, the village, several nearby farms, and a distant lake. A small yellow airplane was circling the grounds as if they were looking us over. I had always wanted to ride in a plane, but right then the Ferris wheel felt a lot like flying, and I was sorry when our seat reached the bottom and we had to get out.

We debated about which ride to try next. I had no trouble ruling out the Tilt-a-whirl after watching some of the passengers try to walk away after they'd disembarked, but the merry-go-round looked inviting and I liked the happy music. We hopped on the colorful horses and went up and down, and round and round with riders of all ages, from a scared child to somebody who looked like my great Aunt Mavis.

With only one dime left, I had an important decision to make about where it would go, but my sister dared me to go on the swings. They looked really scary, but I couldn't ignore the dare so I climbed on and, once again, opened my eyes only after what felt like two turns around. I began to feel dizzy as we swung out over the crowd below, but it was exciting to look down. The happy music of the merry-go-round was so loud it almost drowned out the noisy gasoline engines that powered the rides.

By the time we were let off the swings I was feeling heady and my knees were wobbly, but I recovered quickly and realized how hungry I felt. The smells from the cooking booths were hard to ignore and I was almost wishing I had saved 10 cents for one of the great looking hot dogs on a roll with mustard and relish. But then my brother suggested going back to the car to eat. We headed back through what seemed like a longer Midway than it had been when we walked through it the first time, because now it was even more crowded, Like most farm families, we had brought our lunch, partly to save money but mainly because my family didn't trust "fair food" or the greasy looking people who cooked it. I thought the smells of hamburgers and hot dogs frying, sweet corn, and popcorn were mighty tempting as we walked by the eating stands, however, and couldn't help but envy the people walking past us munching on candied apples and cotton candy, and drinking root beer. But when we reached the parking area in the oval, all around us other farm families had returned to their cars, too, and were eating. When we got to my brother's Ford, we passed around the sandwiches of thick homemade bread filled with wild raspberry jam, hard-boiled eggs, and the raisin-filled cookies. Everything tasted awfully good but I still sort of wished that my bottle of milk had been root beer.

Well-fortified, I wanted to return to the fair quickly, especially because this time my sister and I were to be allowed to go off by ourselves. I wanted to see the Midway once more, but over the loudspeaker came the announcement that the stage show was starting, which the ads, as always, had promised was "bigger and better than ever." Since the grandstand was free to kids, we walked boldly into the reserved section directly in front of the stage where lots of people were already seated, but I wasn't completely sure that we belonged there and expected every second that someone would toss us onto the race track.

No one did, and the show began on the open stage just across the racetrack where some funny clowns cavorted around the stage. The master of ceremonies, dressed in a white suit, began the show by telling some jokes that disgusted the prim looking ladies behind us who said he ought not to be invited again next year. He then introduced a cowboy who sang Red River Valley and some other songs while strumming a guitar, interspersing his renditions with some fascinating rope tricks. In the next act, five dogs did all sorts of tricks, and I wondered if I could teach our Peggie to walk on her hind legs and jump through a hoop when I got home. Then we all gasped as a lady contortionist twisted her body into all sorts of strange shapes and even put herself through a small hoop.

Each fair had at least one spectacular event each year and my sister said the year before it had been a hot air balloon and parachute jump. This year it was a diving horse. A white horse and rider climbed up a ramp to a platform that wasn't as high as they'd advertised, but still it was impressive. The horse hesitated, looked over the crowd, and then, with the pretty girl on his back, dived into a canvas-lined pool of water as the crowd gasped. Muddy water splashed over the young boys standing nearby while we all laughed. It was fun to watch, but I wished I could have seen the hot air balloon and parachute.

I was intrigued with the high-wire performer who carried a small umbrella as she walked across a sagging wire held between poles. It was equally exciting when a man climbed to the top of another tall pole and stood on his head.

I thought that the grandest event of Youth Day at the fair was the parade. Boy Scouts, 4-Hers, church youth groups, FFA boys, and children from many schools marched along to the music of numerous high school and church bands. They all looked snappy in their colorful uniforms and since I had never before heard live marching band music, it sounded exciting. The band from the State Reform School especially intrigued me. Several stern-looking adults marched beside the rather tough-looking young musicians and kept a close eye on them. I wondered, if I should end up in Reform School as my family sometimes predicted, I could learn to play a trumpet like those boys did. All afternoon men carrying baskets and trays went up and down the stairs in the aisles of the grandstand selling hot dogs, candy bars, and soda pop that was packed in buckets of ice. Others were waving small cards and yelling "Score cards for the horse races. Can't tell the horses and the drivers without a score card. Only ten cents!" Sulky horse races went on between the different acts throughout the afternoon. Since there was no starting gate, the drivers, armed with a whip and dressed in dark glasses and colorful satin shirts and caps, sat with their legs spread far apart on two-wheeled carts. They drew lots to determine their starting order, and a man in a high booth near the stage rang a gong whenever a racer made an untimely start, which happened several times before each race was finally underway. At last he hollered "Go!" in a loud voice, and they were off. The horses were trotters, and if any of them "broke" and ran, the sulky was immediately disqualified, which I didn't understand.

Many people seated around us seemed to be familiar with the horses and drivers and, although betting was illegal, it was going on and probably accounted for much of the crowd's enthusiasm. A team of horses pulling a round wooden yellow water wagon round the track was more interesting to me than the sulky races. It sprinkled water frequently to keep the dust down, but the effort seemed rather useless since the hot sun dried the track almost immediately.

As we left the grandstand after the last show to find my brother and his wife, I felt a little sad because we couldn't stay longer. All around us were boys who didn't have to go home to round up cows and do chores. Several men were setting up tall racks of what my brother told us would be rockets, pinwheels, fountains, and firefalls, all part of the nightly display of fireworks which we would miss. When we reached the car, my brother pulled a couple of bottles from beneath it that some drunks had thrown there. I was glad he had, because we saw someone changing a tire as we left the grounds, bumper to bumper, in a line of cars filled with farm families going home.

Another long line of cars was coming in through the gates as we went out. I decided that some year I would surely be there for the grand cavalcade of animals and all the evening events. But for now I was satisfied. It had been quite a day, and I really didn't need any more excitement. The shows and rides and people I had seen raced through my mind like a kaleidoscope of color and noise. I had already decided not to be a dairy farmer, and now I had some thrilling options. Should I become a drum player, a policeman, a cowboy, or perhaps an acrobat?

It was lucky that I had to help with evening chores and had no spare minutes before bedtime to practice becoming an acrobat. On the party line the next day we heard that a young farmer who lived near us had also watched the contortionist. When he got home he had pushed a leg up in back of his head, and his wife had to call in two of their neighbors to untangle him.

Chapter 14

Summer's End

"Shore miss the summer folks. Ain't been half as much to talk about 'round here since Labor Day." Charlie Findley.

According to the Old Farmer's Almanac, summer ended officially on the 21st of September, but for us, it ended on Labor Day. There was no mistaking it. The sun was rising more than an hour later than it did the first of July and setting nearly an hour earlier. Nights had cooled considerably, and by then some years we'd already had a hard frost. The early apples and corn were beginning to ripen. The pumpkins were changing from green to orange, and traces of red and yellow showed here and there on the maple trees.

We could have ignored these harbingers of Autumn for a few more weeks if the town itself had not changed so abruptly when 99.44 percent of the summer people left on or before Labor Day. Now and then a retired couple might stay at the lake for a couple of weeks longer, but since few camps had more than single board construction and only a fireplace for heat, the cold pre-autumn nights and damp, rainy days got them packing. Occasionally a professor on sabbatical and his wife rented one of the vacant homes on the main street for the winter to research or write a book, and their children attended the local school, but that was rare.

With a huge percentage of the population gone, once again our village was quiet and rural. The storekeepers' sales slowed drastically, the minister found many near-empty pews on Sunday morning, and the farmers rejoiced to find, at last, a parking space in front of the stores. My own feelings were mixed. I had enjoyed the summer in spite of the hard work, and I was both anticipating and dreading my first year in high school.

Several events foretold that summer was winding down. The last dance of the season in the Grange Hall always had the largest crowd of the entire summer because everyone, including those who went only occasionally, felt it was important to be there. As usual, the crowd was a mixture of local and summer folks, both young and old. The dances were sponsored by the local Grange every Wednesday evening throughout the summer. They hired a local family band that most natives referred to as 'Harley and His Hogscrapers', and they called the dances 'hog rassels.' The musicians were far from professional but apparently never realized it and would have willingly played at the White House, if invited. None of them could read music, although the piano player propped up some music sheets in front of her so she could see the words and, perhaps, to give the dancers confidence. They were always ready to tackle any new song they had heard on the radio the night before, although their interpretation usually made it hard to recognize. The campers seemed amused by the band's playing, no doubt thinking that it was the local folks' idea of great music. It was a local person, however, who told the Granger who stamped her hand when she surrendered the thirty cents price of admission, "The Grange should really be paying folks to listen to that racket."

The band played square and contra dance music with a flourish, and a man with a heavy French Canadian accent called the changes. "Couples one and tree cross over," he would sing. After two or three sets, the band played a waltz, polka or foxtrot which gave the more professional summer dancers a chance to show their talents, and others often cleared the floor to watch.

The Grange hall was small, and when packed with people, dancing was difficult. The local folks and campers mixed happily on the dance floor. The latter, who might be aloof meeting the farmers in the store, danced among them in the circle dances such as "Soldiers Joy" where everyone moved from couple to couple throughout the dance until the caller instructed everyone to "promenade all to Montreal."

One local couple always made up a little bed on the seats surrounding the hall for their small child who seemed to sleep contentedly through the noise and woke up only when his parents left. Wednesday night was obviously not the child's only dance during the week. He had probably already spent many evenings of his young life at various dances and parties and would probably grow up to be a great dancer after hearing so much music during his growing years.

Some of the younger men came inside only during the dances they liked. The rest of the time they either stood on the porch or leaned on their cars talking loudly. Sometimes they sang lustily cowboy or French Canadian songs, repeating the same chorus over and over. The local constable hired for the dances occasionally came inside, but mostly he strode around outside, wearing a black hat and carrying a long flashlight and a billy club. His job was apparently to keep watch of the drinkers outside and ignore their insults. Both Constable Carson and the boys knew full well there was little he could do, unless he had a really good reason to arrest them.

The intermission started promptly at 11 o'clock and lasted a half hour. Most of the older couples, both local and summer, went home then, even though the dance always lasted another hour and a half. Even after several hours of vigorous dancing, a few energetic young people always went to the public beach for a moonlight swim.

The Grange dances were lots of fun, but there were many others on different nights of the week in the area. Some were in dance halls built for that purpose, and they had lively reputations for fights, car accidents, and sexual encounters. Other dances took place in farm barns or potato sheds during the few weeks when the farmers didn't need them for storing their crops.

At the final Grange dance of the summer, although I knew only a few of the campers at that time, I felt sad to see them leave. For them, too, the evening was nostalgic, and some sang along with the tunes of familiar waltzes or fox trots and called the changes along with the caller. There were a lot of teary goodbyes when the orchestra played 'Till we Meet Again.' "Smile the while, you kiss me sad adieu, when the clouds roll by, I'll come to you..."

Other end-of-summer rituals included picnics. Barr Hill, a local elevation that was once known as the highest cultivated land in Vermont, was a favorite spot. The top was nearly barren of trees after decades of sheep raising and potato farming, but now the summer folks and youth groups who hiked there for picnics and camping shared the stony hillside with a herd of grazing Holsteins. Growing up on the farm meant that we never had time to go on picnics there, even though it was within sight of our house, but at the end of that summer I went for the first time because I had joined the Young People's Group from our church and they had planned a twilight service and hot dog roast.

It was a four mile hike from home, but I hurried through the chores and arrived on time. Our minister was already in the parking lot near the top of the hill with about two dozen boys and girls. Two boys, one from Boston and the other from New York, were with them. They were working on local farms that summer under a government program and enjoying their first encounter with country life.

We all climbed to the summit where we had a spectacular 360 degree view. The lake and the entire village were below us and beyond them were several layers of foothills and mountains in the south and west, with the Green Mountain range in the background. To the east, the White Mountains of New Hampshire towered above the high wall formed by a lower range. In the northeast we could see the small wilderness pond not far from our farm and, beyond it, still more hills and mountains. In the far north, we spotted a hazy elevation our preacher said was Mount Royal in Montreal.

It was difficult to find enough wood for a campfire, because campers had pretty much picked the place clean over the summer, but by searching a wide area we finally found enough to build a small fire for roasting hot dogs and marshmallows on sticks. We never had hot dogs at home so they tasted wonderful, especially with the fresh lemonade the minister had brought. Just as the sun was sinking over the mountains, turning the lake a glowing red, the minister led a brief service and everyone sang "Day is dying in the West..."

After the service we made our way back down the long hill, walking slowly in the dark through a grove of maple trees and edging past the shadowy cows, hoping there wasn't a bull among them. At the foot of the hill we said our goodbyes as we started home in different directions. I still had a long, lonely walk ahead, and it was completely dark as I trudged up the road that I'd soon be walking every day to school, thinking about the hot dog roast, the memorable sunset, and the city boys who were so excited about everything they had found in our town. For the first time, I thought about my State in a completely different light and decided that it wasn't a bad place to live, after all.

Each year we heard about another tradition the younger members of the summer colony enjoyed just before Labor Day. Mr. Young, a farmer who lived close to town, hitched his horses to a wagon covered with hay, and pulled it the 7 miles around the lake with the merrymakers riding in the piles of loose hay. According to some of the residents along the route, the event was always accompanied by considerable drinking and an abundance of noise which usually prompted some of the elderly campers to call the local constable. He dutifully went to the lake road, observed the wagon and the revelers, and, after telling them to simmer down, returned home shaking his head, just as the youths had known he would. Occasionally one of the young people would fall off the wagon, break a limb, and need medical attention, and those years the hayride was widely discussed around town.

No real damage occurred, however, until one summer when one of the boys, who had been drinking, borrowed his father's roadster after the hayride and drove around the lake again with a group of his friends, bashing in mailboxes with a baseball bat along the way. Since wrecking mailboxes was a federal offense, the authorities viewed this sport quite differently than mere carousing. We never heard whether or not the boys were caught and punished, but as far as I knew, none of them were sent to Alcatraz. There was a lot of sputtering by both campers and local folks, and some of them told us they were glad that summer was finally over.

After Labor Day, the local fishermen had the lake to themselves, and quickly took advantage of it. Harvey Rice, a handyman, after landing an especially large fish, was so excited that he spent most of the day driving around town showing it. Finally he stopped at the town clerk's office to ask if there was any way that he could get it officially registered. The clerk, quite bewildered at the request, told someone later she didn't know whether to record it under births or deaths.

September corn roasts, another rite of early fall, were usually sponsored by the church or Grange, but occasionally a local farmer with a surplus of ears would throw a party. The one I went to when I was thirteen was given by our neighbors whose son, Jim, had talked his parents into it. It was a perfect evening for a roast. We gathered just before dark, and the nearly full harvest moon hung low in the eastern sky. The air was brisk but not too chilly, and the crowd was enthusiastic. Unfortunately, Jim had no idea how to get the large pile of wood he had collected to burn properly, and most of it was green and rather wet. So, for the first half hour, while the group stood around looking hungrily at the baskets of corn, Jim was busy lighting matches and blowing on the flickering flames.

About the time we were all wondering if we should go home and get a snack, Jim's dad came with some kerosene, and the fire blazed high. We stuck the corn, still in the husks, on the sharpened sticks Jim had cut, and soon the aroma of burnt corn mixed with the smell of blazing kerosene. Unfortunately, Jim's dad, who had a lot of thrifty Yankee blood pulsing through his arteries, had provided mostly corn that was over-ripe and rather tough. Few of us knew anything about how to roast corn, so the ears were either burned to a crisp or nearly raw. Jim's sister had brought salt, which she passed around, but no one had thought of butter.

We all told Jim and his Dad how good it tasted, but it seemed to me that a couple of bushels of corn had been wasted. I thought it might have tasted better if they had boiled it in a big kettle in a sort of cannibal ceremony, and wondered if I would ever quite understand all our local traditions.

Labor Day week was not only the end of summer but also the beginning of school. Like most eighth graders who had been all 'grown up' in our tiny one room schools, I dreaded starting high school where I would be the youngest and at the bottom of the heap. Unlike some of my friends whose parents saw no need for further education, I had been offered no vote in the decision about going on to more schooling. I worried that the high school would not only be too big for me, but also that there were three teachers there to keep an eye on us instead of only one. We had all heard, too, about the dreaded initiation the senior and junior boys gave the freshmen, leading them to the outlet of the lake and, holding each by the feet, dunking their heads into the cold water. Clearly, my new school was nothing to anticipate with pleasure.

I got a lot of advice about the school from my older brothers and sisters who had gone there. There were usually only 40 or so students in the four grades, but it was large in comparison to our one-room school with a population of ten. The year that I started, however, education beyond the eighth grade had become more popular, so instead of eight or ten freshman, my class had 20. The building housed, in addition to the high school, the village's graded school-one room of about 30 fifth to eighth graders, taught by a single teacher, and another of about the same size with grades one to four, managed by another young woman. During lunch hour, when most of the hundred or so students in the building were ready to drink out of the school's only water fountain in the hallway at the same time, it could be a long wait.

It didn't seem fair to me that the grade school pupils all rode to school in various cars, vans, and trucks called school 'buses', but those of us in high school, except for three elite seniors who drove cars, had to walk even though we had far greater distances to go. We were expected to be there, no matter what kind of weather, and school was never canceled for snow, hail, or epidemic. Since the mileage was doubled if I returned to school for an evening event, it was obvious right from the start that I wouldn't be able to take part in most extra-curricular activities.

The first day, as I started out, I was joined by Leonard, another freshman, who lived north of us. He had already walked a mile and a half and, like me, had three more miles to go. We speculated about what lay ahead, and how to handle it. Many students would be country kids like us, we knew, but the village kids had already spent eight years together in the building, which would definitely give them a great advantage, we figured.

When we arrived I tried to size up my new schoolmates just as they were scrutinizing us newcomers.. Although I was 13, it surprised me that some of the others didn't act that much older. I learned that they listened to the same radio shows that I did-Buck Rogers, Jack Armstrong, Tom Mix, and other programs I had assumed were only for little kids. Even more surprising, some were wearing the adjustable whistle rings, badges, and other items we could get by sending in a dime and a cereal boxtop.

There were many things to get used to that first week. I had to buy books for five classes-English, Science, Latin, Algebra, and History-as well as other supplies. The town did not furnish books, pencils, pens, paper, or any other necessities. On my limited budget, I felt lucky that some sophomores were offering their old books at bargain prices, and even though some were tattered, I snapped them up. The school sold ruled paper, 50 sheets for five cents, but we had to buy our pencils at the general store.

Like the teacher at my one-room school, each of the three full-time teachers kept very busy. The principal, Mr. Noyes, also taught English, Latin, geometry, and algebra. The science and history teacher coached baseball and basketball, and the home economics teacher taught French, one English class and directed school plays. An agricultural teacher came only for the mornings, and spent the afternoons in a school in the next town. Agriculture was a popular course because it was worth two credits and there was seldom any homework. I didn't intend to be a farmer and was one of only eight boys who skipped that course.

The anticipation of the dunking in the lake was worse than the actual event, even though the water was icy cold and it took a long time for us to dry out on that cool fall day. One of my classmates, upon returning to the school, asked the principal if that now made him an official member, but Mr. Noyes only smiled. Fortunately for future freshmen, the tradition of hazing at our school ended with our initiation. The following fall there was only one senior boy, and the rest of us had little interest in helping him continue the ceremony.

I missed the morning and afternoon recesses we'd had in grade school, but there was a long lunch hour because many village kids went home to eat. Most of us took our lunches in paper bags which we piled together in the hallway when we arrived in the morning, and had to sort out at noon. The home economics class provided a hot lunch and during the winter, a few kids bought them. They complained bitterly that the beginning cooks created food that was terrible. The cocoa had either no sugar or too much and was usually cold, and the soups were too salty or created of doubtful materials.

On sunny fall days a few juniors and seniors went to the beach at the lake to smoke during the lunch hour, and the hardier boys even braved brief swims in the cold water, making sure we all heard about their courage for the rest of the day. The rest of us ate outdoors on warm days and at our desks in the classroom when the weather was rainy or cold. After lunch we sometimes shot baskets in the town hall above the school which served as a gym, or played games in the yard.

A few weeks after school began, our science teacher decided to start a mandatory physical education program during a free period. Those of us who did chores and had already walked several miles to school felt that additional exercise was hardly necessary, especially since the teacher had recently graduated from a military college, and his physical education plan consisted of endless military drills. Luckily for us farm boys, after Christmas vacation he became involved with basketball and forgot about the project.

My friends and I who lived on farms outside of the village felt that our teachers, who lived only a few hundred feet from the school, could never understand those of us who had to work in the morning, then wash, change clothes, and walk for an hour or more to get there. They continually urged us to take part in plays, operettas, and other evening events. Because there were so few boys, the teacher who coached basketball pressured us endlessly to join the practice after school each day and then play two evening games a week with other schools. They didn't understand that we had difficulty finding enough time to do the unfamiliar homework they so generously assigned.

With a larger percentage of the town's eighth graders going to high school, no one seemed surprised that five of my classmates quit the first year. Many farmers saw no value in having their children learn any more than how to read and cipher. If a boy or girl really wanted an education, their fathers often made it really difficult for them. Bill Bradley's cousin from another high school told him that one day the father of a girl in his Latin class dropped in to check on what was happening. The group was working on the verb amor, and one was chanting: "I love, you love, he loves, etc." The farmer yelled from the back of the room, "If that is what you're learning in this gol ram place, by gory, you're a goin' home, and you ain't never comin' back." He grabbed his red-faced daughter, and her higher education ended on the spot.

On the farm in September we shifted gears. Labor Day signaled it was time to get in the harvest. We dug the potatoes, carrots, beets and turnips and put them in bins in the cellar. We also dried and threshed the beans, and collected butternuts to store in the shed chamber. My mother filled the racks in the cellar with glass jars of the corn, beets, and applesauce she had canned.

I didn't mind a bit eating the boiled sweet corn, early turnips, and delicious pumpkin pie that my Mother concocted each fall, but I didn't enjoy her traditional New England boiled dinner. Everyone in the family except me relished it, but I thought that when six vegetables were all cooked together, it spoiled the taste of each one. The boiled dinner was inevitably followed, for several days, with red flannel hash, a mashed-together concoction of the boiled dinner, heavily colored by the beets. To my mother's dismay, I much preferred an unhealthy peanut-butter and maple sugar sandwich.

In September she reversed her spring duties and took out of storage the heavy wool clothes she had packed away in May, airing them on the clotheslines to lessen the mothball scent. This ventilation was only slightly effective and, like all our neighbors, we smelled like mothballs for several days after cold weather arrived. Somehow she found enough quilts and blankets for each bed. I helped my brothers haul the parlor stove in from the barn where it had been stored over the summer. On the first cool, rainy day we started a fire in it, the beginning of a long winter of trying to keep warm.

As the campers left for the city, many donated clothing, food, games, appliances and other things for the annual fall rummage sale at the church. It was held during school hours so I couldn't go, but some of my family always went, as did almost everyone else in town. They came home with clothes, plus such nifty things as board games, puzzles, and alarm clocks. Once my sister bought me a tennis ball and a slightly twisted golf club, apparently thinking I should begin to learn some of the city folks' games. A schoolmate who wanted to be a Nazi found the perfect brown shirt at the sale, one year. I think he wore until it fell apart, or the war began, whichever came first.

Much of our fall shopping we did out of the Sears Roebuck and Montgomery Ward catalogs. Both firms sent us a fat book twice a year. A spring and summer one arrived in late winter, and the fall and winter version came in late summer. During the year we also received numerous sale catalogs, including a medium-sized Christmas edition filled mostly with toys.

As soon as the new fall catalog arrived my mother began figuring how much of our limited resources would go toward long underwear, wool pants, and heavy shirts. I studied the pages carefully with an envious eye, knowing we couldn't afford any of the things I really wanted in the so-called "Wish Books".

Since the new merchandise was out of my reach, I spent a lot of time perusing an old 1900 Sears and Roebuck catalog that my family had kept. It was hardbound, and unlike the regional catalogs that now came from Boston and Albany, this one had come from Chicago so it covered the whole country. In it were windmills, saddles, chaps, and other equipment for the West, as well as gaily decorated pot-bellied stoves, pitcher pumps, hand-cranked washing machines and wringers, music boxes, cider mills, tombstones, sawing machines, buggies, forges, and much more.

My schoolmates and I spent hours looking over the shooting section which covered more than 40 pages. We longed to fill out the order blanks for a double barreled shotgun for 8.95 or an air rifle for 64 cents. Prices of the real rifles began at 3.90. The catalog featured paint in 50 gallon barrels as well as in smaller amounts, claiming you could paint a two story house for $9.10. The music department covered many pages and contained everything from pianos, $87.00, and organs, 46.80, to band instruments such as cornets for $6.65. Some accordions begged to be bought for 1.85, and one violin, complete with case, bow, and instruction book was offered for $2.95. Large roll top desks went for 12.95 and beds for 1.39. Home butchers could find everything they needed there, and for family entertainment there were phonographs, records, stereopticons and pictures, and magic lanterns run by kerosene. Smokers could chose from pages of pipes.

In late September each year, after all the other fairs were done, some of our more adventuresome neighbors drove 50 miles to the famous Tunbridge Fair in central Vermont. Posters billed it as Vermont's World's Fair, but all of us knew it as "The Drunkards' Reunion." The event was reputedly a free-for-all with few restraints, and Mr. Whitcomb, a regular visitor, told us, "Everything you ever heard about it is absolutely true." One of the requirements to get in, we had heard, was that you had to be drunk, or swear before a notary that you would be within 20 minutes. Another requisite was that a man should only appear with some other man's wife. One old farmer told folks he went mostly for the flowers. "My favorite is Four Roses," he reported. His neighbor, not to be outdone, said he went for the poultry show. "I am very interested in Old Crow." Both drinks were popular whiskies in those days.

Stories abounded about the fair, though many were undoubtedly not true. We heard that one night, when things got out of hand, the sheriff and a deputy rounded up a crowd and took them to the county clink. When the sheriff got back to the fair he noticed his gun was missing so he called the jail to see if they had found it. The jailer went in to check with the inmates. "Yeah, I've got it," one man confessed drunkenly as he handed it over. "I thought there was a good chance he might hurt hisself, so I took it off him."

I thought the fair sounded even more exciting than our county fair, but it was impossible to go when we were in school, even if we had the money. Only a few boys in the Future Farmers of America agriculture class were allowed out of classes for such events, so that hopefully they would pick up a few farming tips. The rest of us struggled with our Latin, English, algebra, science, and history.

The beautiful romance with the girl that I had seen on my grade school picnic in the spring and longed for over the summer didn't develop when I became a freshman. She already had a boyfriend her own age, but I did occasionally get a smile from her. I didn't mind much after classes began, though, because I was already becoming hopelessly infatuated with my beautiful English teacher.

One day in history class the first week of school someone slipped me a mushy note from Sally Merchant, a very fat girl. Then, a few minutes later, I got another from Sue Smith who was cross-eyed and seemed slightly goofy. Passing notes seemed to be quite a sport in this new school and, since I wanted to be polite, I felt I had to respond to the ones I received. Unfortunately I hadn't yet learned the skills required for successful note passing. The teacher saw mine as it traveled along the row of desks, and made me go up front and read it aloud while everyone laughed. Like my first day at the one room school I had left behind, there was a lot to learn here. I could only hope that things would go better after I had picked up a little more expertise.

About the Author

Lewis Hill and his wife Nancy have had 15 books published by Knopf, Storey Publishing, Stephen Greene, Globe Pequot, and Rodale Press. They have contributed to numerous other publications including the Organic Gardening Encyclopedia, Wise Garden Encyclopedia, and others. They have also furnished articles for many magazines including Horticulture, Country Journal, Harrowsmith, Organic Gardening, and National Gardening. Their book, Secrets of Plant Propagation was chosen as one of the 75 best garden books written in the past 75 years.

The Hills have been the recipients of many awards including the Quill and Trowel award given by the Garden Writers of America, and the Certificate of Appreciation given by the Eastern Nurseryman's Association. They are Vermont natives and have operated nurseries in the Northeast Kingdom for over 50 years. They live in the Northeast Kingdom in Vermont, where they write, garden, and experiment with plants, having developed and introduced nine new daylily hybrids, two new currants, and two new elderberry cultivars.

Printed in the United States
2888